READING: A HORSE-RACING TOWN

by Nigel Sutcliffe

About the author

Nigel Sutcliffe was educated at Reading School, followed by three years in the RAF and a career in banking. On early retirement, he took up his hobby of sports journalism on a full-time basis for local newspapers. His main interests are horse racing and rugby football.

Published in the UK in 2010 by
Two Rivers Press
35–39 London Street
Reading RG1 4PS
www.tworiverspress.com

Two Rivers Press is a member of Inpress

Designed by Nadja Guggi
Map by Geoff Sawers

Printed and bound by Imprint Digital, Exeter

ISBN 978-1-901677-68-3

The Earley Charity
by hook or by crook

Two Rivers Press gratefully acknowledges financial assistance from the Earley Charity

Acknowledgments

First and foremost I would like to thank Tim Cox for the use of his superb library in researching this book and his kindness in dealing with my queries. Thanks also to William Morgan whose information about the early days of racing at Reading proved invaluable.

David Cliffe and the staff at the Reading Local Studies Library were always extremely helpful in dealing with my queries, while John Dearing and John Goodwin, among many others, were of great assistance.

I am also grateful to Adam Sowan and Barbara Morris of Two Rivers Press for their guidance along with Nadja Guggi for her enthusiasm in the lay-out and design of the book.

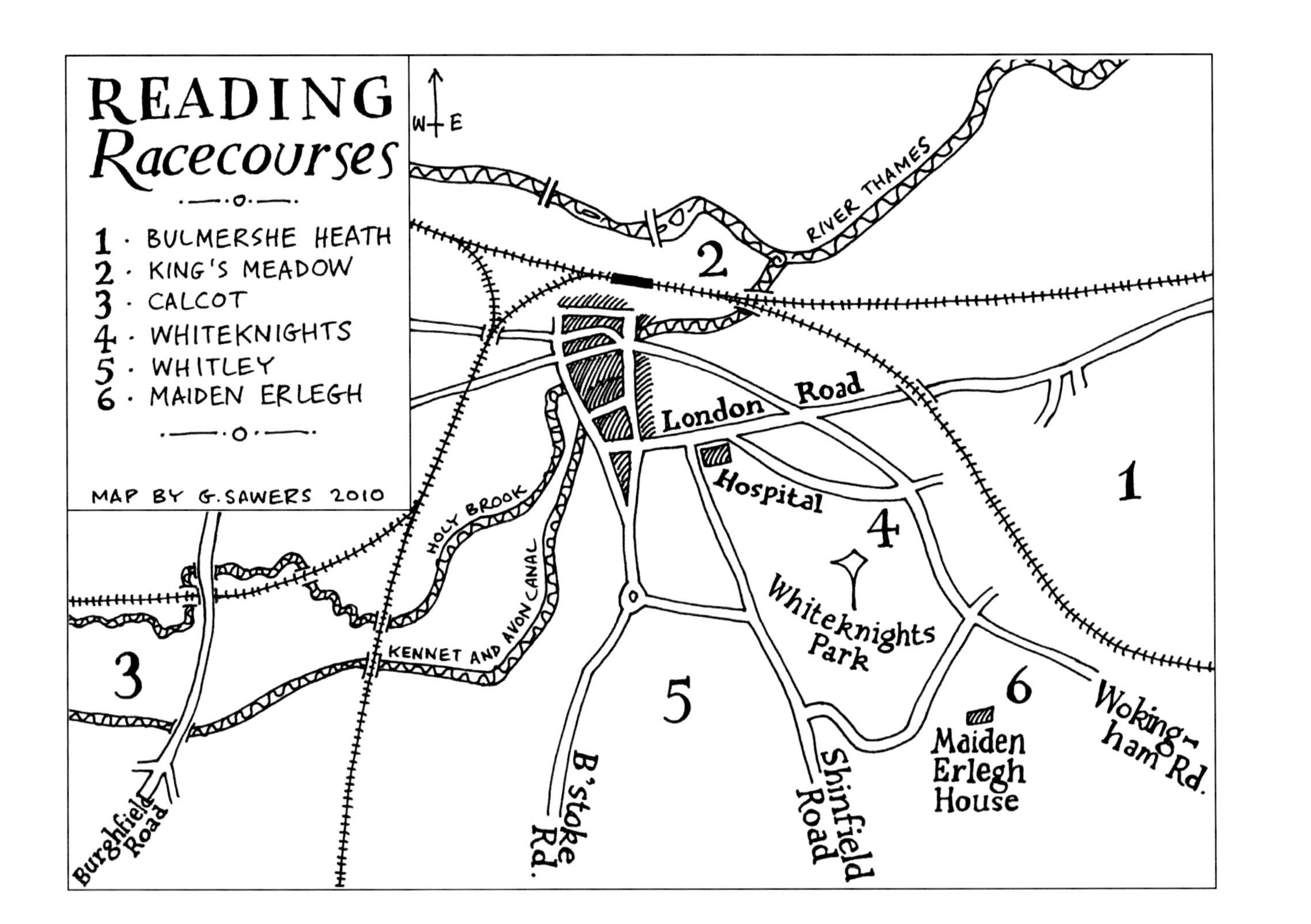
READING
Racecourses
1 · BULMERSHE HEATH
2 · KING'S MEADOW
3 · CALCOT
4 · WHITEKNIGHTS
5 · WHITLEY
6 · MAIDEN ERLEGH
MAP BY G. SAWERS 2010
W E
RIVER THAMES
London Road
Hospital
Whiteknights Park
HOLY BROOK
KENNET AND AVON CANAL
Burghfield Road
B'stoke Rd.
Shinfield Road
Maiden Erlegh House
Wokingham Rd.
1
2
3
4
5
6

Contents

Introduction

Reading never became a major venue for horse-racing, though at one time it did vie with Ascot. Yet for over a century up to 1814 the sport was held at Bulmershe Heath on the eastern outskirts of the borough, followed by spells at King's Meadow, Calcot, Whiteknights, Whitley and Maiden Erlegh. As racing only took place on a few days each year, there were no permanent stands; there is nothing now to be seen at any of these sites, nor do any of them appear on any published map. Several famous horses raced at Bulmershe, including the well-loved little grey *Gimcrack* which won there in his unbeaten debut year of 1764. Enclosure of common land meant the end of racing on the Heath, now part of the suburb of Woodley. But after a break of 30 years, flat meetings took place again on King's Meadow, close to the town centre – and steeplechasing at four courses continued into the 20th century. King's Meadow enjoyed a fair standard of racing, despite rather ordinary facilities, and top jockeys rode there, including champions George Fordham and Fred Archer. Fordham completed a five-timer in consecutive races one afternoon in 1864, and Archer rode a treble ten years later on the way to his first jockey's title. It was at King's Meadow that Reading Football Club played their first ever game, against Reading School, in 1872.

Opposition by religious bodies, plus the activities of criminals, ended horse-racing at the riverside track, and part of King's Meadow racecourse is now buried under a modern residential and commercial development. On the bend where

Archer booted home his winners now stands the fruit and vegetable department of a Tesco superstore.

After the closure of King's Meadow then Whitley, the only local races were jump meetings organised by the Garth and South Berks Hunt; and in 1886, racing under National Hunt Rules was established at Maiden Erlegh, a couple of miles east of Reading. This was on the estate of James Hargreaves, subsequently bought by diamond magnate and famous racehorse owner Sol Joel. The death knell of organised racing in Reading came in 1906 when Joel decided to turn his attention to breeding and set up the Maiden Erlegh Stud. The estate eventually became the site of a comprehensive school in the 1960s.

Any account of horse-racing, in Reading or elsewhere, is bound to contain a great deal of social as well as sporting history. Much of the interest arises from the combination of high life (the aristocracy and their race balls) and low life (crime and corruption). Actual racing took up only a small proportion of race days, so there was plenty of time for other entertainments, eating and drinking, gambling – and picking pockets.

Bulmershe: horses on the heath

The start of racing at Bulmershe Heath is lost in the mists of time. But the first mention of the sport, 'on Early and Bulmershe Heaths' is in a **1705** copy of the London Gazette. The races were apparently on common land and adjacent heathland which had become Blagrave property in the 16th century, when Robert Blagrave's widow Agnes married William Gray. He owned significant real estate in the Reading area and purchased the Manor of Bulmershe for £246 in 1546. When he died it was inherited by Agnes and Robert Blagrave's son John.

That 1705 advertisement gave notice of two races on the Heath – one each on 9 and 10 August. They were a 20 guineas contest for horses which had not won £30, and a 10 guineas Town Plate for horses whose prize money had not reached £5. The horses carried eleven stone over a trip of four miles, with three heats in each race. This was the usual distance at the time; horses had to be shown at the King's Head in the Market Place a week before the racing. The course was three miles round. No Gazette advertisement was published in **1706**, but a single plate of a 'full value of £10' was offered on 2 October **1707**.

During the early 18th century there were many local, country meetings operating in the area – Abingdon, East Ilsley, Lambourn, Newbury, Wantage and Windsor – but most of them were intermittent affairs. Reading and Ascot were two of the few with any continuity, and Reading in particular was an ideal spot for racing. It was easily accessible and a busy town with plenty of local aristocracy to support the sport.

Results for Reading Races appeared for the first time in **1727** when John Cheny issued his first 'Historical List of all Horse-Matches run, and of all plates and prizes run for in England.' This was the forerunner of the Racing Calendar, which is still published today. Jockeys' names did not appear in the calendar until the 19th century, but those of owners did. Many horses were ridden by their owner or a stable lad not worthy of mention as it was considered the four-mile races run in heats required no particular skill. The early stages were at no more than walking pace before the speed quickened towards the finish.

Racing began each day around 4 pm and rarely consisted of more than one race, usually run in three heats. A horse which won two would be declared the winner; if the three heats were won by different animals, a fourth would be run for which only the three winners would qualify. A horse which did not win but was inside the distance pole – 240 yards from home – as the winner passed the post was said to have 'saved his distance' and was allowed to compete in the next heat. If horses tied for first place, the heat was held to have 'died' – hence the modern expression 'dead heat'. It would be re-run. Sometimes there was a 'match', a two-horse race, usually between members of the landed gentry.

There were plenty of other entertainments besides horse-racing during the week, including boxing matches and fairground activities, and in certain taverns in Reading cock-fighting, not yet outlawed, proved popular.

The first day's racing in 1727 was an event worth 30 guineas – free for horses carrying 11 stone which had never won £50. It was rather a damp squib as none started except Mr Heathcote's bay gelding *Plain Dealer*. The next day a purse of 15 guineas was competed for by galloways (a breed of Scottish pony) which had never won £30. A weight of ten stone was the highest 'give and take', a type of handicapping in which weight is allotted according to size. Under this system a horse standing 15 hands would carry 11 stone, while one measuring 14 hands significantly less. The race was won by Sir Thomas Reynell's *Merry Batchelor*, successful in both heats and thus carrying off the prize. On the third day Mr Buckworth's grey gelding *Wanton Willy* took both heats of the Hunters Plate.

From that year, Reading Races was an annual feature in Cheny's List except for 1735 when, for no apparent reason, details were omitted. But from then on results of racing at Bulmershe were published without interruption for over three-quarters of a century. In **1736** the £30 race went to one of the best galloways of the time, Lord Weymouth's *Flush*, subsequently owned by Lord Portmore and renamed *Young Cartouch*. He was considered an outstanding animal before the thoroughbred became established and was given a place at stud.

Parliament introduced legislation in **1740** to limit racing. Prize money had to be a minimum of £50, which led to the disappearance of many smaller meetings; but Reading managed to survive, while Ascot struggled and did not race for four years. Reading races were usually held between early July and September, although in the early days there seemed to have been no fixed spot in the calendar.

Mr Grisewood's *Partner*, with 20 victories behind him, won the £50 in **1743**. He was a veteran of 12-years-old and quite lame. At the same meeting, *Starling*, bred by John Croft at Barforth in Yorkshire, was starting an illustrious career. He also won races at Oxford and Chippenham, and the following year took a valuable event at Newmarket before going on to triumph in King's Plates at Guildford, Salisbury, Winchester, Canterbury, Lewes and Newmarket. King's Plates were introduced by Charles II and there were 15 by the middle of the 18th century. Those courses making a meaningful contribution to the country's bloodstock staged these prestigious races, which attracted a better quality animal.

After victories at Newmarket and York, *Starling* won four further races in **1746**, including a match over four miles for 200 guineas against Mr Parsons's *Babraham*, a horse with an interesting pedigree which had won the Plate at Reading. This horse was bred by Francis, second Earl of Godolphin, and sired by the famous *Godolphin Arabian* which, along with the *Darley Arabian* and the *Byerley Turk*, made up the trio of

READING—Berks.

On the 28th of *August* 50l. was run for, carrying Wt. for Age, which was won by

	H. 1.	H. 2.
Mr. *Rickett*'s Chef. H. 5 Yrs. old	1	1
Mr. *Bever*'s Bay H. aged	2	2
Mr. *Stone*'s Bay C. 4 Yrs. old	3	dr

On the 29th, 50l. was run for by 4 Yrs. old Colts, wt. 8ft. 7lb. Fillies 8ft. 4lb. and won by

	H. 1.	H. 2.
Mr. *Green*'s Gr. C. *Gimcrack*	1	1
Mr. *Hawes*'s Chef. F.	3	2
Ld. *Castlehaven*'s Chef. F.	4	3
Ld. *Portmore*'s Br. C.	2	dr

On the 30th, 50l. was run for, Give-and-Take, 14 Hands, aged, Wt. 9ft. higher or lower, Wt. in Proportion, allowing 7lb. for every Year under 7, and won by

	H. 1.	H. 2.	H. 3.
Mr. *Marshall*'s Bay M. *Diana*, Wt. 9ft. 8lb.	4	1	1
Mr. *Tate*'s Gr. H. *Punch*, Wt. 8ft. 11lb.	1	3	2
Mr. *Johnson*'s Chef. H. *Trinket*, Wt. 8ft.	2	5	3
Mr. *Heath*'s Bay H. Wt. 7ft. 10lb.	3	2	4
Ld. *Castlehaven*'s Chef. M. Wt. 9ft. 7lb. 8 oz.	5	4	5

Unbeatable: Racing Calendar records *Gimcrack*'s success at Reading in 1764

founding sires. All modern thoroughbreds trace their descent from these three through the direct male line.

Around this time 'sportsmen' whiled away their time in the morning with cock-fighting. A popular venue for this pursuit was Sacheverel Barnham's cockpit at the Golden Bear Inn in Castle Street. In the evenings there were assemblies – dinner-dances – at the Town Hall, so every hour of the day could be filled with some activity for the racegoers who flooded into town. Prize-fighting, although illegal, also attracted plenty of interest and support, especially from the aristocracy. During race week taverns in Reading provided 'ordinaries' – a meal prepared at a fixed rate for all comers.

In **1747** on Tuesday these were at Mrs Braventon's Upper Ship in Duke Street, on Wednesday at Mr Fisher's Black Bear, Bridge Street, while Mr Askey's New Inn provided Thursday's fare. Lunch was on the table at 2pm each day, racing beginning usually a couple of hours later at the Heath just over three miles east of the town centre, between what is now Wokingham Road and Crockhamwell Road. Around this time, a notice appeared in the Reading Mercury warning that selling liquor on the Heath was forbidden during races, unless the vendors gave at least five shillings towards the Plate. This had to be paid to the Clerk of the Course before the day's sport began.

Top horses frequented the Heath and left with the prize-money. One of these was Josiah Marshall's highly-rated *Little Driver*; described as 'the strongest and best of his size that was ever bred in this kingdom', he recorded a success at Reading in **1750**. He won the £50, the seventh victory of his career. He also took the prize-money in 1751 and 1754, around which time August meetings became the norm.

Disputes were commonplace and in **1753** a race took place which figured a century later in the book 'Horse Racing' by the great racing reformer Admiral Rous, in the chapter on Racing Cases. It concerned Mr Sparrow's *Badger* in the £50 Plate over four miles. As *Badger* failed to arrive in line for the first heat, the stewards agreed that he should start for the second heat if he performed the distance by himself in 9 min 20 sec, which was the time *Poor Robin*, under 10 stone 5 lb, ran the first heat. But *Badger* failed to complete the four miles under ten minutes and was deemed distanced.

There was more controversy in **1760**. At that time there was a rule in racing that jockeys could only dismount when permitted to do so. Consequently Mr Clarke's grey gelding was declared distanced in the Hunter race after winning the first heat.

One of the most famous horses in racing history ran at Reading on the second day of the **1764** meeting. The grey *Gimcrack* won an event for four-year-old colts and fillies worth £50, finishing first in both heats of a four-horse race in his unbeaten debut year. The four rivals he overcame in the heats were unnamed – merely Mr Hawes's chestnut filly, Lord Castlehaven's chestnut filly and Lord Portmore's brown colt. *Gimcrack* also had successes that year at Epsom (where he won a £50 plate), Guildford, Winchester, Bedford, Barnet and Burford, mostly in four-mile and two-mile heats. He beat the top horses of the day including *Hazard, Lass of the Mill* and *Lady Thigh*.

Past master: *Gimcrack* portrayed by George Stubbs

Gimcrack's memory is preserved with the annual running of the Gimcrack Stakes at York, a top race for two-year-olds. The winning owner has the honour of making a speech at the Gimcrack dinner, and in 2001 that task fell to Manchester United boss Alex Ferguson after the success of *Rock of Gibraltar.*

The stewards for **1769** were Lord Cadogan and John Dodd, and entries were to be made at the Black Bear on Bridge Street. That year cock-fighting took place at the Cross Keys on the corner of Gun Street. During race week 31 cocks were produced by the gentlemen of Oxfordshire and Berkshire at four guineas a battle, though the side bets could have been far higher.

There were years when runners on the Heath were few and far between, and **1770** was typical. A three-heat race on the Tuesday went to Captain O'Kelly's chestnut mare *Davy-maid.* O'Kelly, a colourful character, arrived in London as a penniless and illiterate 20-year-old. But with the financial backing of a notorious brothel-keeper, Charlotte Hayes, he became a successful gambler. He also purchased one of the most famous horses in racing history, *Eclipse*, which was unbeaten in 18 races.

Wednesday's four-year-old plate was cancelled, as only two out of four entered horses appeared at the post after the fillies of Mr Bailey and Mr Adams had fallen lame in the morning. On Thursday racegoers were disappointed yet again because of a lack of horses qualified to run for the Give and Take plate. Messrs Weatherbys, the emerging administrators of racing, issued a statement before racing showing their increasing influence on the sport. It read: 'No horse, mare or gelding, the property of Mr Castle, or his son, or of Mr Quin, will be permitted to start for either of these purses.'

The history of Bulmershe Heath is peppered with tales of accidents. *Chaffinch*, a runner in the £50 race on the Wednesday of the **1774** meeting, broke out of the course and knocked down 'a poor labouring man' who received a severe bruising. A collection was immediately organised, and happily he recovered. Racegoers went to meetings on horseback and mingled with runners in the home straight; very little, if any, of the course was fenced off. Stricter safety measures in racing were not introduced until the early Victorian era. Some spectators could not resist accompanying the runners down the course – sometimes at a faster pace than the participants. There is even an instance of a father riding alongside his jockey son throughout the race, giving advice.

Trouble broke out in **1775** as soon as racing ended on the last day. A riot ensued between 'gentlemen on horseback and the foot people' after an assault on one of the riders going to weigh-in. Two people ended up in Reading jail, and in the Berkshire Chronicle the event was celebrated in verse as 'The Battle of Bulmershe Heath':

The Heath resounded with the clatter,
Of whips and sticks which heads did batter,
Gingerbread, apples, Bottle ale,
And salmon, flew as thick as hail;
At length when ammunition fail'd,
The benches from the booths they hal'd.
And at their adversaries hurl'd,
To send them to the other World.

Sir Charles Bunbury, along with Lord George Bentinck and Admiral Rous, was one of the most influential members of the Jockey Club in the first 100 years or so of its existence. During his time the five Classics were introduced, and he had the honour of owning the first winner of the Epsom Derby, *Diomed*. One of his lesser-known horses, the bay colt *Fortunio*, ran on the Thursday of the **1783** Reading meeting but could only finish third, third and fourth in the heats of the four-year-olds' £50 race.

Planning of fixtures was rather haphazard, and in **1784** the races scheduled to begin on 12 August were postponed until the end of the month because meetings had been arranged the same week at Burford, Egham and other courses. Entry of horses was to be on a revised date of 27 August between 4 and 7pm at the Broad Face Inn, High Street, a pub which no longer exists. There was only one entry, Mr Broadhurst's *Rosaletta*, for Tuesday's race, so it was abandoned. On the Wednesday Mr Wynch's *Little John* won both heats, and the following day Sir Frederick Evelyn's bay colt repeated the feat.

Spectators witnessed skullduggery on the opening day of **1786**. A match for 50 guineas took place between Mr Hilton's dun mare *Miss Tiffany* and Mr Frogley's horse. After one circuit of the course *Miss Tiffany*, the favourite, had the race well in hand when Richard Bullock from nearby Sonning rode onto the course and knocked down the mare, who was subsequently awarded the race by the stewards. It came to light that Bullock was the real owner of Frogley's horse and had wagered a considerable sum on the outcome of the race. In an eventful week, one of the criminal element was arrested on his way home to Lincolnshire from the races. William Marshall, 30, was detained at the Feathers Inn, Wallingford, on suspicion of fraud through offering a draft in payment for goods at several shops in the town. The draft was drawn by a Mr Gleed of Shillingford on Mr Green of Pangbourne for £6.5s.

A horse, a jockey and a racegoer had a lucky escape in the second heat of the Tuesday race in **1787**. *Merry-Andrew* was brought down while in the lead after colliding with a woman standing on the course. The rider was catapulted a long way, and fortunately, like the spectator, suffered only superficial injuries. On the social side, an advertisement for the Reading Race Assemblies stated that 'great inconvenience arises from payment being made at the door, as it occasions much delay and adds to the difficulty of collecting a proper account of the names of Ladies who choose to dance Minuets.' In future, entrance was to be by ticket only, obtainable at the Post and Printing Offices and at the Horse and Jockey, Castle Street: Gentlemen's Tickets 1787–1792 6s; Ladies 3s 6d.

Mrs Philip Lybbe Powys, a socialite of the time, lived at Hardwick House near the Thames-side village of Mapledurham. She kept a diary around this era, and several entries referred to the events in race week:

> 27th August 1787: Went to Reading Races. The last ball a very brilliant one.
>
> 20th August 1788: We went to my mother's at Reading for the race-time. Miss Ewer met us there. The races not good, the balls tolerably full, considering how many families at this season leave their seats in the country for the different watering-places now in vogue. The middle day went to the play, Thornton's company being then in town. [Henry Thornton, actor-manager, opened Reading's first purpose-built theatre in this year.]
>
> 24th August 1789: We all went to Reading for race-time. Lord Barrymore was steward. Of course the sport was good, and assemblies brilliant. We were at the last only.
>
> 23rd August 1790: My brother went to Lord Camden's, and we to my mother's at Reading for the races and ball. Caroline for the first time.
>
> 28th August 1792: The Reading Races. The middle night we were at the play, 'The Child of Nature', and 'No Song No Supper'. We had been at the races the first day, and we set off for the course this too, but unfortunately were overturn'd, or I may say fortunately, as neither my poor mother, Caroline, or myself were the least hurt. Caroline and I at first thought of not attending the theatre after this accident, but in the space of an hour or two we had so many inquiries, and report, as is generally the case, had made us all

> suffer such a number of misfortunes, that we determined to show ourselves alive and well; so had the glasses of our coach mended, and enter'd the playhouse, to the infinite surprise of all our acquaintances, and received such numerous congratulations as were quite flattering.

The Lord Barrymore mentioned as steward at the **1789** meeting was Richard Barry, 7th Earl of Barrymore (1769–1793), a close friend of the Prince Regent and known as 'Hellgate'. Richard was one of four children of the 6th Earl, who were all given nicknames to suit their individual traits. His sister Caroline was called 'Billingsgate' because of her use of foul language, his brother Henry had a club foot and became 'Cripplegate', while another brother Augustus was 'Newgate' because it was alleged that was the only prison he had not been in. Richard, a proficient jockey, set up his own stables as a teenager, and managed to fritter away over £300,000 of the family fortunes on horse-racing.

When he obtained the appointment of steward for himself at Reading, almost the whole sporting world turned their back on the course and no horses were entered for the Plates. This meant he was forced to enter his own horses in the names of friends to avoid embarrassment. He also advertised a £50 Plate to be run for by hunters, then ran a Newmarket horse of his own in the name of a dependant to win it for himself. His other major interest, besides 'hell-raising', was the thespian world; he built a luxurious theatre at Wargrave, a village near Reading, where he put on plays for his friends. He died at the age of 24 in a shooting accident when a loaded gun, left leaning against a carriage seat, went off.

Illegal gambling was rife in race week: on Tuesday evening of the **1791** meeting an E. O. table, a form of roulette used at the races, was seized at a private house in Reading and destroyed. The owner was kept in prison overnight but released the next morning after 'promising to alter his way of life'. Safety on the course continued to be poor, and regular reports of accidents appeared in the local press. On the Wednesday Mr Whiting's filly collided with 'a countryman's horse' while on the Thursday

Hellgate: Lord Barrymore, the Georgian tearaway

three horses, *Straggler, Britannia* and *Andromeda,* fell after colliding with a cow which lay on the course. John Halladay, the rider of *Straggler,* sustained life-threatening injuries.

A member of the Royal family had to settle for second best on the Heath in **1792**: The Prince of Wales's *Devi Sing* was runner-up to Mr Hamond's *Minos* in a sweepstakes of 25 guineas each. During the races at Bulmershe, horses were stabled at the inns in Reading. King's Meadow, the site of the Reading racecourse some 50 years later, was used as gallops.

Appropriately the Horse and Jockey, still standing on Castle Street, was the pub where entries for the **1795** meeting were accepted between 4 and 7pm on the Monday the week before the meeting. The fees were 'three guineas to the plates and five shillings to the clerk of the course or five guineas at the post and ten shillings and sixpence to the clerk or whom he shall appoint'.

As occasionally in previous years, the **1796** races were marred by a lack of runners; in fact they proved to be a fiasco. On the Tuesday the £50 weight-for-age was won by Mr Stapleton's *Susannah,* as Mr Hallett's *Hum* fell lame in the first heat and was distanced. The next day, neither the £50 event for four – and five-year-olds nor the £50 race for three-year-olds was run, only one horse being entered for either. Only two horses went to post for Thursday's handicap plate – Mr Dundas's *Jack of Newbury* and Mr Stapleton's *Susannah*. The first heat was won by *Jack of Newbury*, after which Stapleton wished to withdraw his mare, but was asked by Dundas to run her to entertain the spectators. The plan backfired as *Jack of Newbury*, after about a mile of the second heat, dislocated a coffin joint and never ran again.

There was bad luck in **1797** for John Lade in a race for three-year-olds. His grey colt by *Pilot* fell at the start, throwing his jockey, who immediately remounted and gained lost ground on the other riders. But it was not to be his day. He was obstructed by a horseman riding across the course and ended up being distanced. Crime was rife on the Heath, and many pickpockets were plying their 'trade' on the course each day. They were out in force on the Thursday when a French immigrant priest (one of several hundred who had come to Reading to escape the Revolution) was robbed of a gold watch. The culprit, of distinctive appearance, should have been easy to trace. He was 'of middle size, between 40 and 50 years of age, had only one eye, his hair cropped; he had on an iron-grey coat with a black collar, black waistcoat and blue stockings'. A guinea was offered for recovery of the watch.

For the **1803** race meeting an advertisement in the local paper stated that 'all persons who intend to erect Booths, Stands etc are desired to meet Joyner Becher, Clerk of the Course, at the Chequers, Bulmershe Heath, to take their ground and pay for the same, and no stands, booths, carts, tables etc to be allowed without his consent.' In a rather forlorn attempt to avoid accidents, it went on: 'by order of the Stewards all dogs seen on the course during the races will be destroyed. All persons are desired to keep out of the lines while the horses are running, and whoever interrupts the persons appointed to keep the course in the execution of their duty, will be prosecuted.'

The Chequers pub, reputed to have been over 500 years old, was pulled down in 1962, and another hostelry of the same name was built in its place in Crockhamwell Road, Woodley.

There was yet another fixture mix-up in **1805** when Reading races clashed with those of Newbury's opening meeting on 19 August, and the latter was moved to September. Mr Congreve's *Quiz* triumphed at 3-1 in the inaugural Gold Cup. This was a top racehorse which ran for seven years and on his second outing as a three-year-old won the St Leger at big odds. At that time he was owned by a clergyman, the Rev. Henry Goodricke, but for obvious reasons he ran under the name of Mr G Crompton. The Reverend, however, died just after the St Leger victory; *Quiz* went on to sire *Tigris*, the 1815 winner of the 2,000 Guineas.

There was a tragic accident the following day when an 18-year-old girl named Harrington, the only child of a Reading tradesman, was knocked down while crossing the course with some friends and died soon afterwards from her injuries. It appears that the two sons of Edward Golding of Earley (Maiden Erlegh) Court were racing their horses in an unauthorised contest without the knowledge of the Clerk of the Course when the accident took place. Golding, MP for Downton in Wiltshire, had accumulated a huge fortune from the East Indies and used much of it to buy Maiden Erlegh and other property in Berkshire. He was Lord of the Treasury during the administration of Henry Addington, Viscount Sidmouth.

Misfortune struck again in **1806**, happily with less serious consequences, when *Langton*, hot favourite for the second running of the Gold Cup, met with disaster when making his run in the straight. Because of lax security – no Health and Safety then – he collided with a large coach-horse which was being ridden across the course by a gentleman's coachman. *Langton*'s rider remounted, but the horse could hardly raise a gallop and was distanced. Neither the coachman or his horse were injured. *Langton* recovered and was set to run in the next meeting at Egham.

In this year a spoof Reading Races card was used for political purposes in the run-up to the General Election later in the autumn. Frances Annesley, who had been elected six times as local MP, was described as 'the grey horse Perserverance, aged, runs well, has won no less than six plates.' Mr Shaw Lefevre

READING RACES.

A Subſcription Match of One Thouſand Guineas each p. p. will be run for at our next Races, by the following Horſes, named by their Owners.

Mr. Anneſley's *grey horſe* Perſeverance; aged. Perſeverance was got by Mr. Vanſittart's *Nabob*, out of *Aurora*. He is a fine horſe of his hands, *runs well*, has won no leſs than *ſix plates*, and was *never beaten*.

Mr. Shaw Lefevre's bay horſe *True-blue*, five years old, got by John Bull's *Constitution*, out of Mr. Simeon's Miſs *Haughty*. He beat his antagoniſt *hollow* at our laſt races; goes in *grand ſtyle*, and is conſidered by the Amateurs, a *good-bottomed* horſe.

Mr. Simeon's *pye balled* horſe *Coaxer*, nine years old. He was got by Mr. Neville's roan horſe *Deſerter*, out of *Ambition*. Coaxer *never won* a plate, except once, when he *walked* over the Courſe. He is apt to be *reſtive*, and at our laſt races was very *unwilling to ſtart*. At that time Perſeverance *took the lead*, and True-blue kept within *half a neck* of him the whole of the way, but Coaxer *bolted* ſoon *after ſtarting*, then run on the *wrong ſide the poſt*, and being hard preſſed by his rider *broke down* in the firſt round, by which many of the *knowing ones* were taken in. Theſe in conſequence of their *diſappointment* blamed the rider for ſuffering himſelf to be *out-jockeyed*—the rider laid the fault on the groom for *letting him eat* a large quantity of *grains*, which he ſaid had ſo *blown him up* that he was not *fit to run*, and the groom exculpated himſelf by proving that the principal cauſe of his breaking down was his *carrying his head ſo high, he could not ſee his way*.

Great Sport is expected on this Match.—Even betting on Perſeverance.—Six to Four on True-blue, and Three to Five on Coaxer; provided the *grains* are kept *out of ſight*.

*** *An Ordinary as uſual after the Race.*

E.ᵈ B.ʸ *Clerk of the Courſe.*

Aug. 23, 1806.

SNARE AND CO. PRINTERS, READING.

Spoof racecard: Aimed at the local contestants in the 1806 General Election

was termed 'a bay horse True-blue, beat his antagonist hollow at our last races, goes in grand style'. Severe criticism was directed at John Simeon. He was 'a pye-balled horse Coaxer by Deserter out of Ambition. He is apt to be restive and unwilling to start'. (It was alleged that Simeon's wealthy brother Edward had paid for the erection of the obelisk in Reading's Market Place in an attempt to influence voters.) The card was printed by Snare and Co on 23 August, a few days before the races at Bulmershe Heath, where it was probably distributed.

Around this time a gushing report appeared in a Reading newspaper:

> Our races were as numerously attended and offered as much diversion, as we have remembered in some years past. The ordinaries, which were sumptuously supplied with the best viands, excellent wines and the finest fruits, were crowded with persons of the first respectability and distinction. The balls, and the theatres, were graced with the most brilliant assemblage of beauty and fashion ever beheld, particularly the ball and supper on Thursday evening, which was exceedingly grand. At one, the company sat down to the splendid supper, consisting of every delicacy the season could afford, together with the choicest fruits that could be procured, and above all, the unremitting attention of the stewards, to anticipate every wish of the company, who testified their utmost gratification and enjoyment. It may be truly asserted that no public entertainment of this description has ever been exceeded, or rarely equalled in this or any other public place. About two, the company returned to the ballroom and numerous fashionable parties did not leave the festive scene until Phoebus had risen far above the horizon. Great praises due to Mr Trendall, who conducted the entertainment with his usual judgment and attention.

After the **1807** races the Marquis of Blandford, who had been appointed a steward for the next year's meeting, entertained lavishly at his palatial Whiteknights home. He organised a grand fete complete with a marquee for the assembled company which included his lordship's friends, officers of the First Reading Volunteers, and 'a great number of inhabitants of the town'.

The visitors were treated to a series of military exercises by the Volunteers under the command of the Marquis, and afterwards enjoyed 'a cold collation consisting of every delicacy of the season'. Blandford leased the property from family trustees, but five years later it had to be mortgaged to pay off his debts incurred 'through scandals and some ill-conceived ventures'.
He spent enormous amounts on art, books and exotic plants.

Mr Dilly's black colt *Japan* won the £50 plate for three- and four-year-olds at Bulmershe in **1810** and went on to even better things at Royal Ascot the following year, where he lifted the Oatlands Stakes. The race had been introduced in 1790 and was a landmark in English racing. It was the first handicap in which horses' weights were adjusted according to form – and it carried huge prize money. *Japan* triumphed over five rivals at odds of 7-2. But he could only finish second the following year at Reading behind *Sunbeam* in the All-aged Stakes.

There were wild celebrations on the Thursday evening of the **1812** meeting. News came through of the Duke of Wellington's victory at the Battle of Salamanca, a vital success in the Peninsular War, when it was said that the Iron Duke's men beat an army of 40,000 in 40 minutes. A report in the local newspaper told of

> rejoicings which had taken place in this and the neighbouring counties ... continued at the Assembly on Thursday evening; the room was brilliantly illuminated in appropriate devices, and crowded with a blaze of beauty; wines excellent.

Racegoers were disappointed on the opening day of the **1813** races when Mr Dundas's famous horse *Romeo* had no opposition in the Gold Cup and walked over. Two days later, in a busy week for Dundas, a card-sharper on the course lost £4 to a boy, whom he refused to pay. Dundas intervened when racegoers took the culprit, Michael William Bryant – a licensed hawker from London – to a pond to be ducked. Bryant had a number of forged banknotes and was arrested. His companion Jane Baldrey was also committed for playing dice unlawfully. Dundas, incidentally, was victorious on the Wednesday with his chestnut colt by *Meteor* which won the three- and four-year-old Stakes race. Mr Eade's chestnut horse *Accident* pulled off a four-timer over the three days; he won a

50 guineas match on the Tuesday, and in a similar contest the following day overcame Captain Hervey's *Hunting Bob* after taking a £50 Handicap Plate, winning both heats. On Thursday he accounted for four rivals in a £5 Handicap Plate, again finishing first in each heat.

William Silver Darter, in his 'Reminiscences of Reading, by an Octogenarian' (1888), recalled:

> The races were well supported. The Captain of our Troop of Yeomanry (Captain Montagu) used to invite Fuller Craven and others of his old comrades when he himself was in the Regulars, and drove four-in-hand to the races, usually accompanied by a keyed bugle player seated in the rear.

The year **1814** was the final meeting at Bulmershe Heath after over a century of racing, and what turned out to be the last Gold Cup went to Mr Batson's *Dorus*, who beat *Mountebank* and *Jesse*. The Wednesday's sport had been poor, and the horses entered for the Plate were so badly matched that the stewards would not let them start. It was also a bad time for two pickpockets, who were caught in the act and suffered the usual punishment of being 'severely ducked' by racegoers in what is still known as South Lake. However in the evening the Race Ball proved a great success, with 320 people sitting down for supper.

The demise of racing at Bulmershe Heath was announced the following summer in the Berkshire Mercury:

> In consequence of the Subscription for the Reading Races being so very inadequate to the Expenses, the Races must necessarily be discontinued for the present year. Signed H P Powys, J S Breedon.

As a replacement there was donkey racing at the Forbury; so that according to the anonymous author of 'Reading Seventy Years Ago' (1887) 'so noble, so humane a sport might not sink all at once into oblivion'. And to maintain the social side and at the request of several families, a Ball and Supper was to be held in honour of the Prince Regent's birthday on 11 August. Admission: gentlemen 12s; ladies 10s 6d.

The Blagraves sold the common land at the Heath to Henry Addington, the future prime minister; at the turn of the century he sold the manor on to James Wheble, who enclosed and planted it in 1816. Although the racing disappeared, Wheble allowed the South Berks Yeomanry to drill there; cricket matches also took take place at the Revel, which consisted of contests for prizes. These included bowling for a cheese, ploughing matches and cudgels – a violent sport in which the two participants had to draw blood from each other's head. Mary Russell Mitford's book 'Belford Regis', a thinly-veiled account of life in Georgian Reading, gave a clear message that the authoress was not in love with local racing. In the chapter 'Belford Races' she wrote:

> The races ... the most trumpery meeting that ever brought horses to run for a plate ... are, I am happy to say, a non-existing nuisance. The only good that I ever knew done by an enclosure act was the putting an end to that iniquity. The Heath ... was a dull, flat, low, unprofitable piece of ground, wholly uninteresting in itself and commanding no view of any sort. This ugly piece of ground numbered among its demerits that of being the worst race-course in England.

Miss Mitford goes on to criticise many aspects of the Races in her book, published in 1835; but would she feel any better disposed towards King's Meadow, the new venue for horse-racing in the town eight years later?

The sport of King's Meadow

Nearly 30 years elapsed before racing was revived in Reading, and during that time the town had begun to emerge as an industrial centre. The Great Western Railway had reached the town three years previously, and with a population of some 20,000 it was expanding quickly. It seemed Reading could become a serious rival to Ascot, and public response to the first meeting on Wednesday 16 August **1843** was beyond the wildest dreams of the organisers. Contemporary estimates vary but a crowd of between 7,000 and 10,000 were at King's Meadow despite heavy rain in the morning. The course was ideally situated five minutes' walk from the railway station, close to the centre of the town and within easy distance of most of Reading's inhabitants, as the suburbs had not yet spread very far. On the opening day, the gentry and their families drove to the course in carriages and the ladies, as at present-day Royal Ascot, dressed in their finery to add to the scene. All four-wheeled carriages were charged 5s while two-wheeled vehicles were admitted for 2s 6d. Entry was not allowed for saddled horses.

Racegoers were entertained by side-shows which included 'shooting at a target, throwing at snuff-boxes and fortune-telling by gypsies'. The course, a mile and a half round, nestling between the Thames and the GWR line, was flat without any sharp bends and had stands backing onto the river. Looking across the course from the stands, racegoers could see, beyond the railway, the town to the west, the new jail and hospital, and the River Kennet; and to the east, glorious countryside in the direction of Sonning.

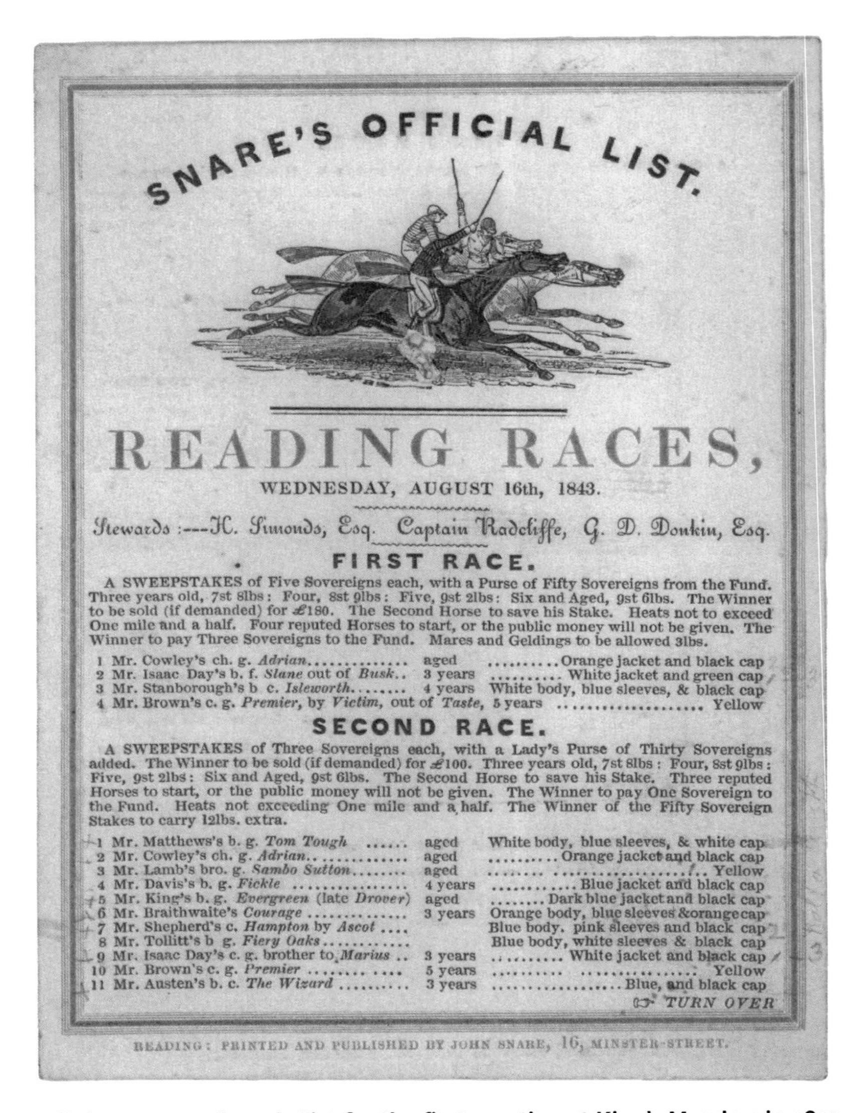

SNARE'S OFFICIAL LIST.

READING RACES,

WEDNESDAY, AUGUST 16th, 1843.

Stewards :---H. Simonds, Esq. Captain Radcliffe, G. D. Donkin, Esq.

FIRST RACE.

A SWEEPSTAKES of Five Sovereigns each, with a Purse of Fifty Sovereigns from the Fund. Three years old, 7st 8lbs: Four, 8st 9lbs: Five, 9st 2lbs: Six and Aged, 9st 6lbs. The Winner to be sold (if demanded) for £180. The Second Horse to save his Stake. Heats not to exceed One mile and a half. Four reputed Horses to start, or the public money will not be given. The Winner to pay Three Sovereigns to the Fund. Mares and Geldings to be allowed 3lbs.

1	Mr. Cowley's ch. g. *Adrian*..............	aged	..........Orange jacket and black cap
2	Mr. Isaac Day's b. f. *Slane* out of *Busk*..	3 years	.... White jacket and green cap
3	Mr. Stanborough's b c. *Isleworth*........	4 years	White body, blue sleeves, & black cap
4	Mr. Brown's c. g. *Premier*, by *Victim*, out of *Taste*,	5 years	.... Yellow

SECOND RACE.

A SWEEPSTAKES of Three Sovereigns each, with a Lady's Purse of Thirty Sovereigns added. The Winner to be sold (if demanded) for £100. Three years old, 7st 8lbs: Four, 8st 9lbs: Five, 9st 2lbs: Six and Aged, 9st 6lbs. The Second Horse to save his Stake. Three reputed Horses to start, or the public money will not be given. The Winner to pay One Sovereign to the Fund. Heats not exceeding One mile and a half. The Winner of the Fifty Sovereign Stakes to carry 12lbs. extra.

1	Mr. Matthews's b. g. *Tom Tough*	aged	White body, blue sleeves, & white cap
2	Mr. Cowley's ch. g. *Adrian*..............	aged	..........Orange jacket and black cap
3	Mr. Lamb's bro. g. *Sambo Sutton*........	aged	.... Yellow
4	Mr. Davis's b. g. *Fickle*	4 years	............Blue jacket and black cap
5	Mr. King's b. g. *Evergreen* (late *Drover*)	aged	........Dark blue jacket and black cap
6	Mr. Braithwaite's *Courage*	3 years	Orange body, blue sleeves &orange cap
7	Mr. Shepherd's c. *Hampton* by *Ascot*		Blue body. pink sleeves and black cap
8	Mr. Tollitt's b g. *Fiery Oaks*...........		Blue body, white sleeves & black cap
9	Mr. Isaac Day's c. g. brother to *Marius* ..	3 years	.... White jacket and black cap
10	Mr. Brown's c. g. *Premier*	5 years	.... Yellow
11	Mr. Austen's b. c. *The Wizard*	3 years	.................Blue, and black cap

☞ *TURN OVER*

READING: PRINTED AND PUBLISHED BY JOHN SNARE, 16, MINSTER-STREET.

All the runners: Snare's List for the first meeting at King's Meadow in 1843

Jockeys were full of praise for the track, especially Toby Wakefield. He had two winners and said 'I never wish to ride over a better course'. There were five races on the cards, all over a mile and a half, one of them a walkover. As at Bulmershe, these were run in heats – still commonplace in those days – which produced a day's racing quite different from the present-day individual races. The three-year-old filly *Slane*, ridden by Wakefield, who sported the white jacket and green cap of owner Mr Isaac Day, had the honour of being the first winner at the new course, taking two of the three heats. In the next race Day and Wakefield completed a quick double thanks to the chestnut gelding *Brother to Marius*. There was a walkover in the third race, yet another sweepstake, for *Norma*; then, to add a little variety, a hurdle race which went to Mr Teales's *Donald Caird*, who took the final two of the four heats. Reading's inaugural programme ended with a Hack Stakes in which Mr Field's *Variety* lifted both heats, the final race taking place at dusk.

The Berkshire Chronicle commented: 'Although no rival to Doncaster or Goodwood, at least it bids to be permanently established on a broad, extended and liberal basis.'

The Oxford Journal was even more complimentary. It read: 'The metamorphosis in the King's Meadow was truly astonishing. That which recently presented itself to the eye as a beautiful and spacious level, now appeared as a compact and commodious racecourse.'

The officials for the day were Ascot clerk of the course William Hibburd, judge, Mr Shirley, clerk of the course, and Mr Richardson, secretary. To round off a successful day, a dinner for 60 racecourse dignitaries was held at the Lower Ship Inn, Duke Street.

There was little criminal activity at the meeting, but an incident in the town between a race-card seller and shopkeeper ended in court. James Hester preferred a charge against Maggs, a linen draper of Broad Street, for jostling him and 'causing him to let his cards fall into the road'. Hester claimed compensation of 6s per dozen – double the sum he would have obtained selling them singly. Hester was unable to prove his case, so Maggs issued a counter-charge against him of creating a disturbance in Broad Street and obstructing the footway. Hester was found guilty, fined 5s and in default of payment sent to 'durance vile', an ancient term for jail, for one day.

Down the straight: King's Meadow, 1844

After the success of the inaugural event, the **1844** meeting was extended to two days as part of a three-day sporting festival in the town. The Reading Regatta was held on the Thames earlier in the week. The Illustrated London News commented:

> Reading has at length shaken off a lethargy of nearly half a century. With the 'long-faded glories' of Bulmershe Heath the name of Reading disappeared from the list of sporting towns. Few persons cared to visit a place, which remained, as it were, shut up within itself, and which seemed to heed so little the good which might be derived from a proper attention to its own natural advantages. Things are altered now; and three days' sport of the first order, show something like a desire and determination to atone for past negligence.

But local civil and religious bodies had a dimmer view of the new, exciting sporting scene. They claimed that 'these new entertainments can only open a new arena to gambling, licentiousness, drunkenness, immorality and cruelty'. Their attitude was of little concern to the racegoers who flocked to King's Meadow, where the attendance was again estimated rather vaguely at between 10,000 and 15,000. The full stands, acquired from Ascot, Epsom and other towns, 'presented a dense crowd of fashion and gaiety'. The atmosphere in the town was becoming similar to the annual Reading Music Festival of the present day, with a huge throng bringing business to local shopkeepers.

William Hibburd took over as Ascot clerk of the course in 1836 and performed similar duties at Reading in **1845**. He had been appointed at Ascot after William IV demanded a shake-up at the course following a decline through poor management. Hibburd was highly regarded in racing circles, and after the Reading races he had been asked by the Duke of Richmond to be clerk of the course and starter at the next Goodwood races. He was also retained for the York races in September.

Meanwhile there were only three races at King's Meadow, one of them in two heats, on the first day of the meeting. No entries were received for the last event, the Innkeepers Plate – disappointing the large crowd. Tommy Coleman's *Devil Among The Tailors* repeated his win of the previous year in the Berkshire Stakes, despite jockey Wakefield putting up at least 12 lbs overweight. Coleman had told Wakefield to force the pace and the *Devil* was suited to the tactics, winning by two lengths. Coleman explained:

> Mine was a light-fleshed, light topped gelding, arch-kneed and with big open feet, and consequently went over and above the soft ground by the Thames side. Those with small feet and straight legs went dibbing into the mud over their hoofs and in some places up to their pastern joints.

Arrangements for the course were changed in **1846**. Stands were increased from six to seven, and booths and stalls were erected on the south side of King's Meadow close to the railway embankment, but this switch deprived ladies of a pleasant walk along the Thames. A match between two local residents, the final event of the day well after 6pm, provided most interest to racegoers on the Wednesday. Mr Cooper's pony *Flora* had been strongly backed against *Gaiety*, a mare belonging to Mr Palmer, a butcher in Friar Street. They started from the winning-post and *Gaiety* took the lead, but *Flora* tracked her until she faded at the final turn. *Gaiety* steadily increased her advantage but her jockey, believing *Flora* to be hard on his heels, 'whipped, pulled and spurred' his mount to finish 100 yards clear, to the amusement of the crowd.

In **1847** the legendary 'Squire' Osbaldeston won the Caversham Stakes with *Cerberus*, in a re-run following a dead-heat with *Moodkee*. George Osbaldeston, a feisty little character, achieved fame in 1831 at the Newmarket Houghton Meeting when he wagered 1,000 guineas he could ride 200 miles in 10 hours. He completed the distance in 8 hours 42 minutes and used 29 different horses, which he changed every four miles. But Osbaldeston had been less successful on the racetrack with his chestnut gelding *Cerberus*, which had finished unplaced four times with the owner on board. The horse fared better with jockey Sharpe as pilot, and after winning the Caversham Stakes he was sold for £250 to Mr Elwes and subsequently to Mr Bray. With new owners, *Cerberus* won three of his six races. The following year Osbaldeston again lifted the Caversham Stakes – this time with *Fugleman*, ironically beating *Cerberus* into fourth place. However on the first day of the meeting there were only three races, run in a total of five heats, and the next day the five-race card included a walkover. The following year Osbaldeston had to sell his estates for £190,000 to repay his gambling debts of £167,000, mostly on horses.

The problems of the 1847 meeting were overcome the following August, and the races attracted grudging praise from the sporting newspapers. Bell's London Life commented in its report of the **1848** meeting:

> Among minor race meetings Reading may now with becoming pride, boast of holding a position second to none; indeed if improvement continues at the rate at which it has progressed for the last two or three seasons, we can see no reason why the 'minor' should be applied. The disappointments which were experienced last year were amply compensated by the meeting. We now have the pleasure to record the entries for the various stakes were good and the fields productive of some excellent sport.

The sting in the tail came when the newspaper criticised the starter and hoped a more suitable person would be found for the job the following year.

The Sporting Magazine was slightly condescending:

> A better sample of rural racing was produced at Reading. They had a couple of days brim full of sport, though the quality was not of a very high average. Heats greatly abounded; but it should be stated, in mitigation of the practice, that at country meetings it is shown to be possible to run races of that description 'on the square' while at more distinguished places they are synonymous with robberies. The first day – reckoning heats – made up eleven races, and the second eight. To be sure a race in four heats loses it flavour towards the dregs, but rural appetites do not stand in need of much pampering.

By **1849** Reading Races had become an increasingly fashionable venue at which to be seen, and many leading local families were present, including the Goldings of Maiden Erlegh in a carriage drawn by four superb horses which attracted a lot of attention. Other notables included W H Stone, J B Monck, R Allfrey and General Pigott plus sporting gentlemen such as Lord Strathmore and Sir John Hawley, who agreed to act as a steward in 1850. The recently elected MP for Reading, J F Stanford, was present on both days in 1849. On being shown the weighing-room by an ardent supporter of his cause, he asked to be initiated into the mysteries of jockeyship, but was curtly told he would need more than one visit.

It was feared that entries would fall short because the Wolverhampton, Chelmsford and Canterbury meetings were being held around the same time, but happily this was not the case. For the first time trains ran on the Reading and Reigate line, making it easier for people from Wokingham, Blackwater and further afield in Surrey to attend. There were fears for the well-being of one of the riders in the first heat of the Borough Plate. On making the turn, *Sister to Pillage*'s jockey, a tiny boy named Barker, around 12 years old, was thrown from his mount. He was immediately picked up by some racegoers and taken to the weighing stand and examined by a surgeon. Happily he suffered just a bruise on the forehead and was fit to ride later in the meeting.

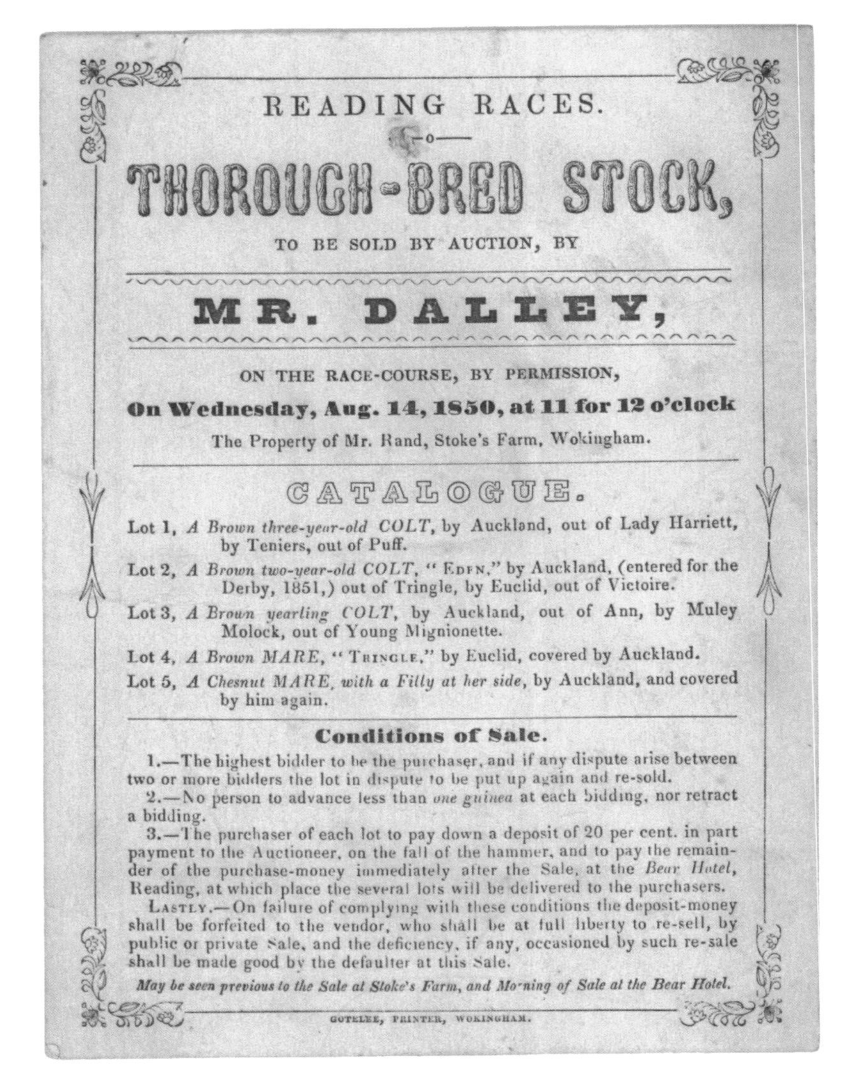

READING RACES.

THOROUGH-BRED STOCK,

TO BE SOLD BY AUCTION, BY

MR. DALLEY,

ON THE RACE-COURSE, BY PERMISSION,

On Wednesday, Aug. 14, 1850, at 11 for 12 o'clock

The Property of Mr. Rand, Stoke's Farm, Wokingham.

CATALOGUE.

Lot 1, *A Brown three-year-old COLT*, by Auckland, out of Lady Harriett, by Teniers, out of Puff.

Lot 2, *A Brown two-year-old COLT*, "EDEN," by Auckland, (entered for the Derby, 1851,) out of Tringle, by Euclid, out of Victoire.

Lot 3, *A Brown yearling COLT*, by Auckland, out of Ann, by Muley Molock, out of Young Mignionette.

Lot 4, *A Brown MARE*, "TRINGLE," by Euclid, covered by Auckland.

Lot 5, *A Chesnut MARE, with a Filly at her side*, by Auckland, and covered by him again.

Conditions of Sale.

1.—The highest bidder to be the purchaser, and if any dispute arise between two or more bidders the lot in dispute to be put up again and re-sold.

2.—No person to advance less than *one guinea* at each bidding, nor retract a bidding.

3.—The purchaser of each lot to pay down a deposit of 20 per cent. in part payment to the Auctioneer, on the fall of the hammer, and to pay the remainder of the purchase-money immediately after the Sale, at the *Bear Hotel*, Reading, at which place the several lots will be delivered to the purchasers.

LASTLY.—On failure of complying with these conditions the deposit-money shall be forfeited to the vendor, who shall be at full liberty to re-sell, by public or private Sale, and the deficiency, if any, occasioned by such re-sale shall be made good by the defaulter at this Sale.

May be seen previous to the Sale at Stoke's Farm, and Morning of Sale at the Bear Hotel.

GOTELEE, PRINTER, WOKINGHAM.

Sale catalogue: Thoroughbred Auction held at King's Meadow, 1850

The presence of large crowds attracted more and more criminals from London, an easy trip on the train from Paddington. Among these were members of the London Swell Mob, described as 'dressed in the height of Cockney fashion, bedizened with mosaic jewellery, and puffing cigars'. One of them was hauled in front of the Reading magistrates. He was

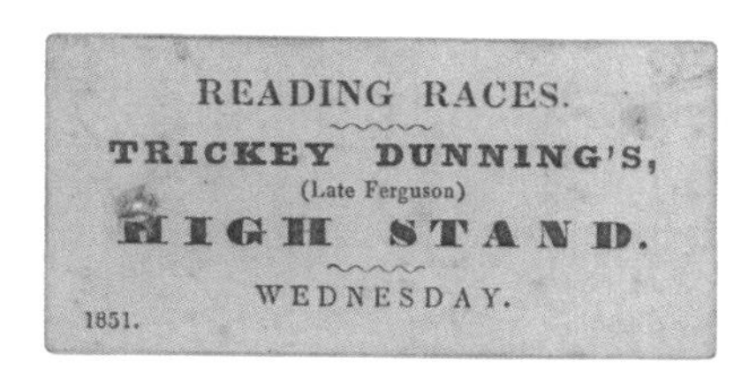

READING RACES,
THURSDAY—1850.
G. CARTER & H. FORD'S STAND.

Wednesday Tickets, 1850/1851: King's Meadow, Trickey Dunning's High Stand; Thursday Ticket, 1851: G Carter & H Ford's Stand

19-year-old Edward Felix, 'a young dashing fellow', charged with being a reputed thief and suspected person, having visited the racecourse to commit a felony, i.e. to pick pockets. He was caught relieving Alfred Wheeler of various items and received one month's hard labour.

As well as the light-fingered brigade, the mid-day mail train in **1850** from London brought a thousand 'turfists', many from Tattersalls, while many other trains were also packed. There was a slight alteration to the course: Robert Clarke's meadow was added to the course for the two-mile race, giving a longer final straight. Lord John Scott's colt *Windhound* won the Caversham Stakes over six furlongs on the second day – and went on to achieve a place in breeding history by siring 1860 Derby winner *Thormanby*. Despite his Reading success, *Windhound* had proved no great shakes on the turf but Scott retained him for his Cawston Lodge stud in Yorkshire, where he stood for 10 guineas in the mid-1850s. When Scott's major sire *Melbourne* began to lose his fertility, *Windhound* took over his duties, and with the great staying mare *Alice Hawthorne* produced *Thormanby*.

Auctions were often held prior to racing, and at the 1850 meeting Mr Dalley sold the property of Mr Rand of Stoke's Farm, Wokingham. There were five lots of thoroughbred stock. These included a brown two-year-old colt, *Eden* which was entered for the following year's Derby but never ran.

Great Reformer: Admiral Rous, a regular at Reading

In **1851** the crowd was down by half because of the Great Exhibition at the Crystal Palace. Many locals took advantage of cheap day railway trips to visit London instead of using their holidays to go to the races. The crowd was slightly bigger on the second day as the races started later 'for the convenience of the sporting fraternity who came down from the capital by excursion train'. One of the stewards at this meeting was Admiral Henry John Rous (then Captain), the most famous of all Turf administrators and reformers. After a successful career in the Royal Navy and a short spell as an MP, he devoted his life to horse-racing. He brought the sport into the modern era and instigated many revolutionary changes, including the first weight-for-age scale. Subsequently in 1855 he became Public Handicapper and attended every major race meeting, diligently watching the runners' performances through a large telescope from the top of the grandstand.

The **1852** Reading races suffered the same fate as Epsom and Ascot: in a miserable summer, it began to pour down early on the first day and continued with only slight breaks the whole afternoon. Despite cheap day fares on the Great Western Railway and even lower ones on the South Eastern via Croydon and Redhill (2s return from London), the attendance was small. The few ladies at the course suffered dripping, mud-spattered skirts, and there were only 20 or so carriages present.

Racegoers sought the refuge of stands and booths, but these provided little protection as the south-westerly took the roofs off. The entrance to the course was a bog and the ground in front of the stands was not much better. During the Berkshire Stakes the rain was so heavy it was impossible to make out the runners. The water splashed up as if the horses were running through a pond.

Another improvement had been made to the course itself, with the winning post being placed about 300 yards nearer the railway station; and the last turn at the opposite end of the meadow switched nearer to Kennetmouth, making a longer run-in. The 'ring' was well attended on each day by well-known sporting gentlemen, but on the second day the wet weather continued and the road leading to the railway arch was ankle-deep in mud; the owners of several carts conveyed passengers over the treacherous ground for a penny a head.

There were fewer visitors from country districts such as Hungerford and Maidenhead in **1853**, but this was more than made up by an increase in racegoers from London. Locals gathered on nearby Forbury Hill to watch the arrival of the train around midday. The press commented:

> We must confess we never saw such an importation of the rougher caste of humanity into any town. The rumour spread and the timid began to feel uneasy not only about the security of the contents of their pockets, but of their personal security after dusk, imagining that a thousand evils would befall our quiet town from this invasion of Cockneys.

William Davies, a Brighton bookmaker, was a regular visitor to Reading Races and did brisk business at the 1853 meeting. He was known as 'The Leviathan' because of his ability to settle huge bets immediately. Earlier that summer he had suffered the latest in a series of disastrous Epsom Derbies when *West Australian* won; Davies had to find £48,000 and only just

Classic winner: *Saucebox*, runner-up at Reading but victorious in the St Leger

managed to settle. He had only £200 left when he went to Ascot two weeks later and won £12,000 on the very first day of the meeting. He retired after Newmarket's Houghton Meeting in 1857, and when he died at the age of 61 in 1879, he was rich enough to make a bequest of £70,000 to enable Brighton Corporation to purchase Preston Park and Manor.

More alterations, especially to the course, were made prior to the **1854** races at King's Meadow. Jockeys complained about the short pull-up after they passed the winning-post. They ran the risk of their horses ending in the ditch or under the railway arch among the stones. The course, which resembled a figure 9, was lengthened to a straight of more than six furlongs thanks to a new bridge over the Plummery Ditch, opening up the adjoining meadows and allowing plenty of room for horses to pull up. Trainers and owners considered that Reading now had one of the best two-year-old courses in England. The turf was reasonable and there was no hill to affect the juveniles.

The previous year's complaints about the accommodation in the Grandstand had also been dealt with by the committee.

A new spacious stand had been obtained from Cheltenham 'at great expense'. It held up to 800 racegoers, but there was criticism in the local press that it should have been sited at a more oblique angle to make it easier to follow the shorter distance races.

Another step forward was the abolition of races in heats. The Berkshire Chronicle commented that this would prevent the public being victims of doubtful practices. Two new races were introduced – the Berkshire Hunt Stakes for gentlemen riders of 10 sovereigns each with 25 sovereigns added, and a Scurry Handicap of 3 sovereigns each with 20 added. The race fund had been increased by £170 from the sale of winners, and the press felt that the money could be used 'to have a new telegraph erected, by which the riders' names as well as the numbers of the horses may be seen; also to give the numbers of the first three horses in each race, as at other meetings'. The attendance proved even greater as there was no clash with Wolverhampton races or the opening of the grouse season.

On the second day, the colt *Saucebox* was beaten into second place in the Abbey Stakes, yet the following year he emerged a shock winner of a classic, the St Leger at Doncaster, the odds at 40-1. He was owned by Wantage trainer Thomas Parr, originally a West Country tea pedlar, who began his racing career on a shoestring. In his early days he had to hide from his creditors in a hayloft. Parr also trained and owned *Fisherman*, a remarkable stayer which won 70 out of 121 races including the Ascot Gold Cup twice.

Facilities at the course were upgraded again in time for the **1855** meeting, including a new stand which was built following the success of one hired from Cheltenham the previous year. This was constructed by Biggs, a local builder, for £400, much of that expense being recovered on the first day of the meeting when up to 500 racegoers paid five shillings each for admittance. The structure was said to be the best ever at the King's Meadow site. The flight of steps in front was steep enough to give a good view of the races, so the upper places remained free of congestion.

On the Monday, the day before racing began, there was such a demand for accommodation that all the rooms in local inns and hotels were taken, and people were put up in private houses in the Market Place and Friar Street area.

However the final race of the first day, the Berkshire Hunt Stakes, received scathing criticism from the Press. It was described as

> another of those exhibitions which make us wish that gentlemen would confine their equestrian exhibitions to the hunting field and leave the racecourse to the jockeys. The race presented the curious anomaly of the owners riding their opponents' horses and upon the winner (ridden by Mr Elwes, owner of the second horse) returning to the scales, he was received with derisive cheers. We regret that so good a day's sport should have wound up so badly.

The third horse, *Vulcan*, was owned by Newbury-born George Drewe, who lived at East Ilsley and was both a trainer and landlord of the Swan pub.

On the second day the appearance of *Rifleman* in the Caversham Stakes caused excitement among the racegoers. The colt was owned by Squire Osbaldeston who, despite his money problems, continued his passion for horses. Before the race a notice was posted on the stand: 'Mr Osbaldeston wishes it to be understood that *Rifleman* starts for this race for the purposes of claiming the allowance for the Biennial Stakes at York.' He trotted round to finish a distant last. Prior to the Caversham Stakes, however, *Rifleman* had looked in good shape and his appearance encouraged large ante-post sums to be invested on him on course for the following month's St Leger. Odds of at 100-7 were offered by the bookmakers, making him third favourite behind *Oulston* and *Lord of the Isles*.

Gemma di Vergy, bought as a yearling by the infamous Dr William Palmer, the Rugeley Poisoner, completed a double in **1856** by winning the Abbey Stakes, over five furlongs, and the Reading Stakes, a race over half-a-mile, a distance no longer run in this country. In the January of that year, at a sale of Palmer's horses, *Gemma di Vergy* had been purchased for 105 guineas by a character called Charley Coghlan, who raced the horse under various names including Mr Bond, Mr Hope, Mr Robson, Mr Woodhall and Mr Craven. The horse had proved a wonderful purchase, winning 18 of its 29 races as a juvenile; it was then victorious on 12 occasions and dead-heating once in 19 races as a three-year-old. His best performance was runner-up in the Ascot Gold Cup. However the horse, trained by Joe Dawson at East Ilsley, brought bad luck to his owners. Coghlan ended up in the Insolvency Court, Lord Waterford broke his neck, and a Mr Roundwood went mad. Sir Lydston Newman then bought *Gemma* for 1000 guineas, and he went on to be a fairly successful sire.

Bad luck horse: *Gemma di Vergy*

Another former horse of Palmer's, *Pole Star*, was entered in the Berkshire Stakes but did not run. The animal, which figured prominently in Palmer's trial, had also been owned by his friend John Cook. The previous year Cook had won £3,000 on *Pole Star* at Shrewsbury races but died soon after – poisoned by Palmer.

Besides *Pole Star*, many other horses scratched because of the entry of *Pretty Boy*, a winner at Goodwood, and at Lewes the previous day. However *Pretty Boy*, at 6-4 on, proved to be a disappointment, beaten by a neck by *Brother to Grey Tommy,* owned by John Drinkald, a great supporter of racing at Reading, who at one time had a private trainer with stables in the High Street at Lambourn. Messrs Saxon and Barber, owners of *Pretty Boy,* had been thwarted by the railway company. They wanted to stay on at the Sussex course after their success in the Lewes Stakes, and try their luck in the Lewes Gold Cup the next day. They tried to get the Berkshire Stakes put later on the card so that they could bring the horse by special train to Reading; but the railway company refused to run a special at the speed required to make the plan practical.

Drinkald's victory was popular with the Reading crowd, who greeted the result with loud cheers. He won a total of £1,500 – £500 in prize money and £1,000 on bets – and Admiral Rous was among his many well-wishers. The next year Drinkald nearly pulled off another great coup in a far bigger race – the Epsom Derby. His *Black Tommy,* starting as a 200-1 rank outsider, was in the lead but pipped on the line by the filly *Blink Bonny,* left eight lengths at the start. Drinkald had shouted '*Black Tommy* wins and nobody else has backed him' as the horses neared the line. But his bets proved in vain, including one for £20,000 to a coat, waistcoat and hat.

On the evening of the second day, several preachers assembled in the Market Place to denounce the evils caused by racing. Local thugs smothered them with flour and roughed them up. The Berkshire Chronicle had no sympathy for the do-gooders and commented 'if they keep offending the prejudices of the people, they must expect this kind of treatment'. These were members of the Open-Air Mission, an organisation of evangelicals founded three years previously by a Christian barrister, John MacGregor, to preach the Gospel wherever large crowds gathered. The Mission claimed that 12 of their number attended the races, were kindly received, and distributed 40–50,000 tracts.

The year **1857** was probably the zenith of racing at King's Meadow. It was estimated that there were twice as many racegoers as the previous year, even exceeding the Ascot crowd on Gold Cup day. Early on the morning of the first day, large numbers of racing

The Demon: George Fordham rode a five-timer at Reading

enthusiasts gathered on the course to watch the horses being put through their paces. Racing was set to begin at 2pm, but just minutes before the start a GWR excursion train arrived, and hundreds streamed down the embankment even as the bell rang for jockeys to mount. Crowd control was virtually non-existent, and at the lower end of King's Meadow people stood across the course until the horses were almost upon them, disrupting one or two races.

Highlight of the two-day meeting was the success of *Hobgoblin* in the feature race, the Berkshire Stakes. *Hobgoblin* had been a miserable failure in the Goodwood Stakes a fortnight earlier, but he redeemed himself for new owner Lord Howth, who bought him from Sir William Codrington straight after the race. Sir William, who had bet substantially on *Hobgoblin* at Goodwood, was disgusted by his performance and agreed to sell the horse for

READING RACES.

SOUTH EASTERN RAILWAY.

ON WEDNESDAY and THURSDAY, 11th and 12th August, 1858, A SPECIAL TRAIN, (1st, 2nd, and 3rd Class), will LEAVE LONDON BRIDGE FOR READING at 9.25 a.m. Arriving at Reading at 11.30 a.m. Returning from Reading at 6 p.m. Arriving at London Bridge at 8.40 p.m.

FARES THERE AND BACK.

Third Class.	Second Class.	First Class.
3s.	**4s.**	**5s. 6d.**

The South Eastern Railway Station at Reading is within five minutes' walk of the Race-Course.

Passengers can be booked from Reading to London by the above Train on Wednesday and Thursday at Ordinary Single Fares.

C. W. EBORALL, General Manager.

London Terminus, *July*, 1858.

READING RACES.

WEDNESDAY and THURSDAY, 11th and 12th AUG., 1858.

SOUTH EASTERN RAILWAY.

RETURN TICKETS AT A SINGLE FARE, will be issued from CROYDON, MERSTHAM, RED HILL, and all Stations on the Reading Branch, TO READING on the above days, by the trains leaving London at 6 30 and 9.30 a.m., and Red Hill at 7.25 and 10.40 a.m., respectively.

Returning from Reading at 6.15 p.m. same day.

C. W. EBORALL, General Manager.

London Terminus, *July*, 1858.

Day tripper: Railway Race Excursion advertisements, 1858

100 sovereigns if his Lordship took the animal away immediately. It turned out to be a shrewd transaction for Lord Howth when *Hobgoblin* obliged at Reading and was subsequently quoted at 10-1 for the Ebor Handicap at York.

The following day the Stand Plate, a handicap over half a mile, attracted 28 runners – the largest ever field for a race at Reading. Edward Hibburd, the starter, took a long time to despatch the huge field, and in the melee *Ceres* struck into the heels of other horses, unseated his jockey and galloped home riderless. *Badsworth* was impeded by the crowd at the distance and finished seventh, while *Jack Sheppard*, a winner the day before, broke down and walked in. The eventual winner was outsider *Grand Duchess* who beat the 8-1 co-favourite *Mabel* by two lengths. A £400 wager had been made on the runner-up.

Rising star Henry Custance piloted home outsider *Rotterdam* in the Caversham Stakes and was rewarded handsomely by a couple of bookmakers. Davies, the Leviathan, gave the 14-year-old jockey a sovereign as did a colleague in the ring. Custance went on to ride five Classic winners, including *Thormanby, Lord Lyon* and *George Frederick* in the Derby, and later in life was starter for the Classic in 1885.

Meanwhile at Reading there were lively scenes in the streets, especially in the Market Place, where noisy list-criers (programme sellers) upset the local residents. On the way to the course through the Forbury there were stalls which included a seller of religious tracts and a gypsy willing to tell the fortune of 'any pretty gentleman' if he crossed her hand with silver. Another trader offered a knife which he claimed would cut of its own accord, alongside a stall selling gingerbread and another where the wonders of the microscope could be seen for a penny.

Spoof racecards were circulated on the Wednesday of the **1858** meeting by an anti-racing religious body, earning the severe condemnation of the Berkshire Chronicle. The paper commented: 'The greatest reprobate on the racecourse would have shrunk from such loathsome blasphemy.' Nevertheless the Chronicle reproduced extracts from the card in its columns:

Official List – published by the Authority of the King of Kings.
Chief Patron: Beelzebub, Prince of the Devils.
Stewards (under the immediate control of the Powers of Darkness):
Mr Drinkwell, Mr Swearmuch, Mr Godhater, Mr Blackguard
and Mr Nogood.
Handicapper: Mr Temptation.
Judge: The Lord God Almighty.
Secretary: Mr Thimblerigger.
Clerk of the Course and Starter: Apollyon, the Destroyer.
Description of the horses:
Mr Justice's Avenger, fleet-footed and swift; and though Reckless
has generally started first, and got some distance in advance,
Avenger has always overtaken him by the time he has got to
the Grandstand.
The Judge has always given Avenger the preference.

The Bulmershe Plate, a new race in **1859**, proved popular and attracted an entry of 64 with 12 eventually running. It ended in a dead heat with Mr J Day's *Chere Amie* winning the re-run against *Clemanthe*. On a busy afternoon, *Chere Amie* had already won the first race on the card, the Abbey Stakes. There were no fewer than eight races on the second day of the meeting, thanks to sporting gentlemen providing additional funds to the clerk of the course for two extra events. However there was criticism of the handicapper Johnson, and it was suggested in the press that 'he ought to travel further south and see the horses more often'.

There was an additional stand for the **1860** meeting, much to the delight of the owners and trainers. This was mainly for the use of the stewards and friends, but in the lower part there was a weighing room and the press room. The Berkshire Stakes was becoming one of the great handicaps in the South, with similar prize money to the Ebor Handicap at York.

There were nasty incidents involving racegoers. *Corfu*, cantering down for the start of the Ladies Plate, bolted into the crowd and knocked down a man called Saunders from Bucklebury, who was taken to the Royal Berkshire Hospital with serious injuries. The jockey, Roper, was unseated but unhurt and subsequently piloted *Corfu* into second place.

At an incident-packed meeting there was yet another accident involving the public. The other drama came as horses cantered down to the start for the Forbury Stakes: young James Abbott of the George and Dragon pub at Three Mile Cross was knocked down by one of the horses, but escaped serious injury. He was one of many who continually crossed the course despite the efforts of the police. The crowd was so dense that for half a mile both sides of the course they stood three or four deep.

An interesting runner on the second day in the Whitley Stakes was *Traducer*, who had finished third in the 2,000 Guineas that year. He was unplaced in the Reading event, but went on to become a famous sire in New Zealand. *Spicebox*, ridden by champion jockey George Fordham, won the opener, the Caversham Stakes. Fordham, apparently a great art-lover, had also been in luck the previous evening. He had been the guest of a gentleman in the area and noticed a picture by Sartoris of some horses which ran on the Beacon Course at Newmarket. After looking at the painting intently for some time, Fordham said to the owner: 'I'll give you forty guineas for it.' 'Sixty and it's yours' was the response. Fordham replied: 'No, I'll meet you halfway. I'll give you fifty and you can pack it up and send it to George Fordham, Lewes.' Deal done.

On the opening day of the **1861** races a star attraction was James Merry's *The Knave*, who won the Abbey Stakes at 3-1 on – but only narrowly. Before the race, he was backed at 1000-10 by Captain Little for the 1862 Derby, but afterwards American racehorse owner Richard Ten Broeck was offering 2000-10. In the event *The Knave* ran better in the Epsom Classic than indicated by his price and finished a creditable fifth out of 34 runners.

King's Meadow continued to attract the masses, and in **1862** the Great Western ran a special from Paddington with 22 carriages packed with racegoers. During the day bloodstock was sold at the course by auctioneer Robert Tompkins and there were plenty of other local traders who benefited from the races. Among them was Mrs George of the Wheatsheaf, who looked after the catering arrangements in the grandstand.

READING RACES will take place on
THURSDAY AND FRIDAY NEXT,
AUGUST the 28th and 29th, 1873,
STEWARDS :

The Marquis of Downshire.	Colonel Hargreaves, M.F.H.
The Marquis of Ailesbury.	Colonel Harford.
Earl Craven.	Captain Machell.
Earl Poulett.	G. Payne, Esq.
Lord Ailesford.	C. Alexander, Esq.
Lord Charles Innes Ker.	T. V. Morgan, Esq.
Sir G. Chetwynd, Bart.	H. J. Simonds, Esq.
Sir C. Rushout, Bart.	T. Simonds, Esq.
Sir Lydstone Newman, Bart.	G. S. Willes, Esq.

J. J. Wheble, Esq.
15 RACES IN THE TWO DAYS.
185 First-class Horses will run in the different Races.
Reserved Ground for Carriages.
No Card Hawking or any offensive Games allowed on the Course.
Racing will commence about Half-past One.
R. TOMPKINS,
Clerk of the Course.

Sport at King's Meadow: Reading Races advertisement, 1873

The Sporting Gazette in **1863** claimed that 'no meeting on the home circuit enjoys greater popularity than that annually held on the King's Meadow on the banks of the Thames, at Reading; and considering other places with far greater pretensions, the success of the present reunion was most reasonable'. But that year also saw the biggest influx so far of the criminal element, described in the local newspaper as 'London roughs'. The fine weather had attracted a large crowd, providing plenty of opportunities for illegal gamblers, prostitutes and petty thieves. The Berkshire Chronicle claimed that 'gambling was carried on in all directions and had the whole of the offenders been captured and detained, they would have nearly filled our County Gaol'. Crimes included one at the station shortly before departure of an excursion train: a passenger lost six sovereigns while falling for the three-card trick, then had his purse stolen from his back pocket. Police Sergeant Fenner, in attempting to make an arrest, had his hat knocked off and his silk handkerchief stolen, showing that violence after sporting events is not just a modern occurrence.

George Fordham completed an amazing nap hand on the first day of the **1864** meeting. Fourteen times a champion jockey, he won five races in succession on *Idler* (4-6), *Lord of the Manor* (4-1), *Fanny* (6-1), *Loafer* (4-6) and *Bally Edmond* (5-2) to complete a 339-1 accumulator. Later in the season, at Newmarket, he had six victories in nine rides, and three years later at Stockbridge he repeated the feat on seven mounts. Four of the Reading races were gained by a head or a short head as the 26-year-old, known as 'The Demon', continued the good form shown in Goodwood week when he piloted home nine winners, including the first three on the Wednesday.

It was reported that 'one gentleman who makes it a rule to back Fordham won £1,000 at Goodwood and Lewes, and almost the same amount at Reading.' Fordham left Reading on Friday night with seven successes under his belt after also gaining victories in the Abbey Stakes on *Lady Egidia* and the Forbury Stakes on *Voluptas*. Fordham, with short leathers, rode more in the style of present-day jockeys and was a great tactician. Often he would lull his opponents into thinking he was pushing along a beaten horse, then come with a late run to snatch victory a few strides from the line. The last race of the meeting – the Caversham Stakes – ended in controversy when an objection to the winner *Nebuchadnezzar* was made by the owner of the second, *Batsman*. This was on the grounds that the race was not judged by Mr Clark, the appointed judge, but by Mr Manning, who acted for him. The case was subsequently referred to the Stewards of the Jockey Club, headed by Admiral Rous, who said the result should stand as the race had taken place in accordance with the Rules of Racing.

The Reading course was in far better condition than the recent Sussex meetings at Brighton, Lewes and Goodwood, thanks to rain in the week and the watering system from the Thames. However, there was criticism from people in coaches that the new swimming bath at King's Meadow interfered with their view of the races. (Incidentally, a later bath at the same location is still causing controversy in the 21st century, with a conservation group resisting its demolition.)

There was also scathing comment from Baily's Magazine about the meeting:

> Reading as usual was the trial ground of the Berkshire stables, but the sport does not improve as it should do. The attendance also is not what it used to be, the *profanum vulgaris* being brought down in such hordes by the cheap trains. The local gentry have been frightened from the course and compelled to confine their patronage to Ascot.

Of course in the days before all spectators paid gate money, the only real income was from the subscribers and those in the stand – in both cases the gentry. So there was an increasing danger of 'no gentry, no races'.

During the year the Reading Town Clerk reported that he had had an interview with Mr Cox, Clerk of the Course, at the suggestion of one of next year's stewards, Lord Portsmouth. His lordship wanted certain permanent improvements to be made to the grandstand, and wondered if the Corporation would help with the financial outlay. After some lengthy discussion the request was turned down, but Mr Cox was told he could do what he liked with the grandstand, provided the race committee continued to pay the rent of £2 per annum.

Lord Portsmouth's concern seemed warranted, and was backed up in **1865** by an article in The Times. It read: 'Reading hardly keeps pace with the times in the internal economy of its arrangements. A shabby wooden stand, more becoming Barnet Fair than the capital of Berks, and the weighing department etc. under canvas, place it much behind some of its younger rivals who cannot boast the patronage bestowed on Reading.' Meanwhile, on the Thursday afternoon of the meeting children from the schools of several dissenting chapels in the town enjoyed their annual treat. As usual it was held on the first day of the races to prevent the kids going to King's Meadow.

Richard Ten Broeck, owner of the legendary American horse *Lexington*, celebrated a double in **1866** – the first year the King's

Meadow meeting was extended to three days, with the addition of Saturday to the usual Thursday and Friday racing. It proved far from successful as people preferred to return home on Friday night.

Ten Broeck, determined to prove the superiority of the American racehorse, had come to England with a string of runners. But the initial plan was doomed as his animals travelled badly, although later imports met with some success. Nevertheless he took on the English bookies to earn a livelihood and received their respect. When he died in the States in 1892, one obituary stated: 'He was the most intrepid gambler that ever backed a racehorse, bucked the tiger or bluffed a pair of deuces.' Ten Broeck's winners at Reading in 1866 were *Usher* in the Caversham Stakes and *Claymore* in the Forbury Stakes (Selling Handicap).

Crime figures continued to climb, and probably hastened the beginning of the end for racing at the Meadow, as a stream of cases were heard by magistrates on the Friday. Thomas Williams, a stranger, was charged with stealing 5s, a silver watch, a pair of trousers, a waistcoat and other articles from Robert Noyce of Letcombe Street. He was sentenced to three months. William Webster and Charles Glenville each received one month in prison for playing cards on the racecourse. For the same crime, plus assaulting PC Handford, Fred Warren got two months. His friend Thomas Jones received two months for assault in default of paying a £3 fine. Three months was handed out to William Layton for attempting to steal a watch at the races. John Grimes, a well-dressed middle-aged man from Cheltenham, was charged with being drunk and riotous in Broad Street. He apologised to the bench, claimed he had been an army officer, and was discharged by the magistrates.

Other local sporting events, even minor ones, seemed to be affecting the crowd. In **1867** the Oxfordshire Journal commented: 'The attendance on the course was not so great as we have occasionally seen under less favourable circumstances as to weather. But we believe there were fixtures elsewhere, especially

Pangbourne Regatta, drawing away some of the usual attendants here.' Despite the lack of racegoers, there was no shortage of runners, and the winner of the Berkshire Stakes, *Bradamante* by *Voltigeur*, went on to win a couple of nice handicaps.

The Sporting Life reported that the sport in **1868** 'was not of a brilliant quality' and gave a hint of another problem facing the promoters of racing at King's Meadow: 'The committee are persevering enough but so strong is the religious opposition in the old town they are unable to make progress through a lack of funds to keep pace with the times'. On the second day *Paris*, an old favourite, won the all-aged Selling Stakes in a canter. The horse had run at almost every course in England and passed through the hands of a dozen owners. It soon had another as it was sold after the race to Captain Christie for 180 guineas. One of the innovations on the course was the installation in the ring of an American tube well sunk to a depth of 11ft. It was in constant use by Messrs Keene and Browne and the other caterers on the course.

The decline continued: 'Asmodeus' of the Standard claimed in **1870** that 'it did not maintain its prestige, for the fields in two or three cases were small, and the company fell far below average.' Apparently the clash with the Nottingham meeting had affected attendance, but a few notables such as Prince Soltykoff, Lord Westmorland, Admiral Rous and Sir Robert Peel were there. The course was moved nearer the river and the stand shifted a quarter of a mile. It was a little cramped, with a sharp entrance to the straight, but the track appeared to satisfy trainers and jockeys.

Separate accidents occurred at the two-day meeting of **1871** – one to a racegoer and the other to a rider. On the Wednesday a young woman was injured in a game of Aunt Sally, in which sticks were thrown at a figurine head of an old woman with a clay pipe in her mouth. The object was to break the pipe, but the girl was struck instead; at first it was thought she had been killed, but she regained consciousness after being attended by doctors. Amateur jockey Arthur Yates – more of him later – received injuries while riding the mare *Sally Sutton* in a

Handicap Hurdle Plate in the last race on Thursday. The animal struck an obstacle opposite the stand and Yates was thrown, landed on his head and was carried unconscious from the track. But the injuries proved less serious than thought. He was taken to Flanagan's Hotel for treatment – and probably a brandy or two.

The meeting survived the £50 minimum value rule, but a further shadow was cast over the future of racing at the Meadow when the Public Board of Health bought a large part of it; by the next year it had become a recreation ground, and there was a danger that the sport would not take place. There was also continued opposition from local religious bodies who lobbied the Board to abandon racing at the Meadow, but thanks to the Borough Council the meeting went ahead. A postscript in the Sporting Times read: 'We feel an expression of satisfaction at the overthrow of the "saints" who would have crushed this meeting altogether.'

An important event took place on 21 February **1872** at the Meadow which heralded association football as a major sport in the town. Reading Football Club played their first ever game here – Reading School providing the opposition. The match finished goalless, and both teams fielded 13 players with the town club 'having a little the best of it'. As one sport emerged, another seemed in decline locally, and a report in the Morning Post commented: 'It is known that powerful local influences in Reading are much opposed to racing and Mr Tompkins, the famous auctioneer of the town, is consequently all the more to be commended for the energetic spirit with which he has sustained a gathering which at one time looked like becoming extinct.' However, the Reading Mercury, which had produced lengthy and rather flowery prose in the halcyon days of King's Meadow, apologised for a lack of space to report the racing at length, and merely printed a brief summary from the Daily Telegraph. From this we learn that the legendary Fred Archer, then aged 15, made his first appearance at Reading and piloted the favourite *Pelerin* to victory in the Berkshire Stakes. It was one of 27 wins from 180 mounts for Archer that summer.

Champion jockey: the legendary Fred Archer rode a treble at Reading

The Grandstand was full for the **1873** meeting, and a telegraph office at King's Meadow was introduced. Several stewards were present and occupied the box set aside for them. Measures had been taken to keep the racecourse 'free of all rowdyism and costermonger enterprises'. There were refreshment booths, some fitted up for dancing, but they were cramped and the local press felt 'the crowds inside must have rendered graceful movements a great difficulty to the best dancers present'. Bills were posted around the course, reminding 'welshers' (a non-PC word for those who failed to pay their debts) that the Thames was nearby, while pickpockets were warned of the presence of London detectives among the crowd. Two of the light-fingered fraternity were pounced upon while making a bare-faced attempt to relieve a gentleman of his watch and chain.

Only one favourite won – *Bedgown* – who in a close battle with *Oceania* lifted the Caversham Stakes in what proved a bad day for backers. Jarvis, the jockey who rode *Valuer* in the Welter Handicap, was ordered to be brought before the Jockey Club at the next meeting, because of the way he rode out the finish.

He was subsequently found guilty of pulling the horse, the 20-1 outsider of three, and suspended from riding for one year from 10 September. The weather improved on the second day, but the attendance barely showed an increase. Once again outsiders were to the fore. There were three winners for jockey Harry Constable on the way to his only championship. His tally of 110 was only three better than the up-and-coming Archer, who had a hat-trick on the second day.

An innovation this year was an Autumn Meeting in November. Chaos reigned: the Open Welter Handicap was re-run following the success of *Schottische* with *Canon* second and *Master Herbert* third. The owner of *Canon* objected on the grounds that the horses were started in front of the post. The objection was investigated and the race was ordered to be re-run, but only four of the 11 runners went to post. After a long delay through the inability of the starter to get the horses off, they returned to the enclosure, when the Stewards consented to the judge changing places with the starter. *Schottishe* won again with *Hermitage* second this time; but the latter's owner objected that the judge was not an authorised official. The Stewards, however, overruled the objection and ordered *Hermitage*'s owner to forfeit his deposit of five sovereigns to the Bentinck Fund – the Victorian equivalent of the Injured Jockeys' Fund.

Tragedy marred the second day of the August meeting in **1874** – which proved to be the final year of racing at King's Meadow. Soon-to-be champion jockey, Fred Archer, was involved in a fatal accident. William Clay, a promising young jockey, riding *Purcelle*, died following injuries sustained in the fifth race of the day, the Forbury Stakes, won by Archer on *Oceania*. The 18-year-old was the son of a trainer at Jevington, Sussex. At the subsequent inquest Robert Jacobs, who took a half day off from his job at the nearby Reading Biscuit Factory to watch the racing, said in evidence:

> I went to see Archer as I had heard a great deal about him. I saw the horses start and soon after Archer took the lead. There were three horses abreast and it appeared to me that the rider of the middle horse wanted to get the lead, when his horse's legs appeared

> to get entangled in the other horses' legs on both sides of him and he fell. The other horses went on. The fallen horse tried to get up, but fell back again on the jockey as he was endeavouring to rise. The jockey did not move after, but the horse got up and galloped away. I immediately went to the lad and raised him on my knee. I assisted in bringing him to hospital. The deceased is a stranger to me. I should think the occurrence was purely accidental.

Henry Ducker, a local trainer, also saw the accident and claimed: 'Barlow and Newhouse were the other jockeys involved. It appeared to me that the legs of the horse the deceased rode got entangled with the legs of the horse of which Archer was the rider.' The verdict was 'Accidental Death'. So it was tragedy for young Clay on a Friday afternoon which had begun so promisingly. He had won the second race of the day, the Wyfold Stakes, on *Cocotte*. Archer went on to become champion jockey for the first time with 147 victories. He retained the title for the next 12 seasons before he too met an untimely end by committing suicide in a state of depression brought on by an illness caused by wasting.

There were several liquor and dancing booths on the ground; and on the course, some banjo men and a pedlar who sold, for a penny, 'an illegal picture of a scene in Arthur Orton's life'. Orton, the Tichborne Claimant, impersonated the lost son of Lady Henrietta Felicite Seymour Tichborne. A court case in 1871, in which he attempted to prove his identity in order to inherit the family fortune, lasted 102 days; in 1873 his trial for perjury went on for 188 days, making legal history. Other vendors at the races gave away religious tracts, and as usual a preacher delivered sermons to the large crowd, while near the entrance to the Meadow there were roundabouts, a shooting gallery and a roulette table.

The final meeting at King's Meadow, later the same year, was the recently-established Reading Autumn Military Hurdle and Flat Races under the patronage of officers from Aldershot and Windsor. A two-day meeting held on Wednesday and Thursday 11 and 12 November, it was low-key affair watched by a small crowd: the weather was miserably cold, and most of the top jockeys and leading bookmakers were attending the big Liverpool Autumn meeting. Six races took place each day, and the honour of being the last winner at the course belonged to Mr W K Walker's *Minnie Warren*. Ridden by Daniels, she won the Hurdle Handicap Plate of 40 sovereigns over a mile and a half. That last race, which drew the curtain down on horse-racing on the flat in the town of Reading, was reported as follows in the sporting press:

> The hurdle plate attracted seven competitors to the post and *Twelfth Cake*, who won so cleverly at the late Brighton meeting, was thought a real good thing. Although she looked like winning at the distance, she died away, and *Minnie Warren*, a very small filly, running gamely, won cleverly by a length but had Mr Shepherd come earlier with his rush on *Hoodwink*, he could have won. The event terminated Reading Autumn Sports, which gave general satisfaction.

The public was informed of the end of Reading Races by a paragraph in the Reading Observer of 28 August 1875:

> Mr Robert Tompkins, who has some years past arranged and managed this meeting, has determined not again to undertake the labour and responsibility attending it, so that the Races will be discontinued in future. Mr Tompkins has sold his lease of a portion of this race ground to the gentleman who has previously purchased another portion of it.

That gentleman was George Palmer of Huntley & Palmers, whose biscuit factory was close to the Meadow. As a Quaker he was no lover of horse-racing.

Under the heading 'A Good End', the Times of 6 September elaborated further:

> It now appears that the Reading race meetings are brought into perpetual termination. They were fixed to held at the end of the week, but the subscriptions to the racing fund were so paltry, and the number of entries so small, that the managing committee deemed it better to give up all responsibility in the matter. The subscriptions have been returned, and the lease of the racing ground has been disposed of to Messrs Huntley and Palmer of the biscuit factory. The grandstand was erected and other preparations

> were being made, but all work is stopped, and the races will be a thing of the past.

The subsequent article in the 11 September edition of the Reading Observer, a staunch opponent of racing in the town, is worth quoting in its entirety for its vitriolic content.

> A small paragraph in our local Reading news last week contained an announcement which has given a good deal of satisfaction in the borough and in a large part of the district round it. The statement was reproduced in The Times the following Monday under a heading which admirably expressed the feeling of all who are concerned for the welfare, the peace and quiet and the good morals of the people. The Times has most honourably distinguished itself of late by its courageous exposure of the demoralisation which, in those latter days, has come upon the old sport of horse racing.
>
> While journals which ostentatiously affect a higher tone in political matters give up their columns to a minute record of 'sporting events' the leading journal has consistently given them less and less importance, and has stood alone in discouraging the spread of race meetings. Theoretically we have no objection to racing. A prettier sight, and in itself, a more innocent sport scarcely exists than that of matching against each other a ground of splendid horses. But in this country, and in the present day, the Turf has to be judged by the associations which have gathered round it.
>
> There are, of course, honourable men connected with it; but they will be the first to admit that they form almost as solitary a group as the righteous Lot and his wife when they sojourned in the Cities of the Plain. The whole institution has become utterly vicious and corrupt. It has not only degenerated into an occasion of the most pernicious gambling, but it has got to be surrounded with every kind and form of trickery. Betting is a trade and race meetings are kept up by professional gamblers much as in the London streets crowds are formed by professional pickpockets.
>
> We do not say that this has been the case in Reading, where some gentlemen of unquestionable honour have taken much trouble and much public spirit to keep the races alive. They have probably thought that the town benefited by bringing it to the

> people who came on race days; and they have mostly likely created a good deal of interest in the horses, which are, in fact, the least important item in the whole gathering. We believe, however, that the discontinuance of the meetings will be a benefit to the town and to the district; and we hope no attempt will be made to revive them. The lease of the ground has been purchased by a gentleman who is not likely to let it for the purpose again. We should, however, be glad to see a substitute for the Races provided in the shape of a yearly regatta. Correspondents in our columns have often called attention to the strange neglect of boating in Reading. We shall return to this subject at a future time; and we earnestly hope that before next summer we shall be able to report that Reading is qualifying itself to take that position in aquatic sports which its situation on the river seems to indicate for it.

So ended racing at King's Meadow.

Steeplechasing: jumping around Reading

Racing over obstacles was held on an informal basis prior to the mid-1800s, and there were hurdle races in the early days of King's Meadow; but the first record of organised steeplechasing in the area dates from **1851**. A match for 25 sovereigns took place between Mr Rhys's bay mare *Kate Kearney* and Captain Tyler's *Bedlamite* on 17 February 'near Reading'. The race was reported in a Steeplechasing Almanack as follows: '*Kate Kearney* fell after running half the distance when *Bedlamite* obtained a strong lead; but falling at the third last fence. *Kate Kearney,* in her turn, got the lead and won easily by five or six lengths.'

Calcot

The inaugural Reading Steeplechases in **1857** were meant to be an afternoon's amusement for local sportsmen between Christmas and the New Year. But when it became known that the meeting was to be organised by top administrator William Hibburd, entries flooded in and the Steeplechases attained a higher profile.

They attracted no fewer than 62 horses for four races, held on the land of Mr R J Webb at Calcot, three miles to the west of Reading. The course was situated between the Berks & Hants railway line (Reading–Newbury) and the river Kennet.

This was a far from ideal spot, but the only site available at short notice. Although flat, it was low-lying meadow land, damp and heavy for both pedestrians and horses. The grandstand was near Burghfield Bridge, on the opposite bank of the Kennet to where the Cunning Man pub now stands. A course was laid out of approximately a mile and a half round with six or seven fences and six brooks or dykes to be crossed. It was extremely difficult for horses, and the fences near the road were so dangerous that the owner of *Abd-el-Kader*, a winner of back-to-back Grand Nationals, withdrew from the open Steeplechase because of the risk to his horse. The meeting was in jeopardy on the morning of Tuesday 29 December, but the fog cleared and attracted allegedly 10,000 racegoers, many coming from London by cheap rail excursion.

The first race, the Calcot Plate, a handicap over two and a half miles, was due to get under way at 12.45pm, but there was a delay of three-quarters of an hour until conditions improved. It was won by outsider *Moetis*, while *West End Pet*, at 3-1, finished alone in the next event, the Berkshire Hunt Steeplechase, open only to horses ridden by gentlemen, farmers, tradesmen and their sons living within 20 miles of Reading.

There was a thrilling finish to the Berkshire Open Steeplechase (Handicap) in which Mr John's *The Minor* beat Mr Reynold's *Old Dog Tray* by half a neck. The meeting closed with the Selling Stakes Chase – another outsider *Fanny* getting the better of *Miss Chesterfield* by three lengths.

Whiteknights

After just one year at Calcot, Reading Steeplechases were switched to a more suitable course on farmland in Redlands, between Whiteknights lake and Alfred Sutton School on Wokingham Road. Basically it was a circuit round Edward Chinnock's farm buildings. The course, described in great detail in the Berkshire Chronicle, began in Mr Hobbs's meadow with straight galloping for a quarter of a mile to the first fence, a bank about three feet high with a hedge about two feet on top, then over another grass field in which was placed a flight of hurdles, before entering a small fallow field, running parallel with Whiteknights. Then the horses went into a grass field to clear a brook about 15 feet wide, with a fence in front. After three meadows came Chinnock's farm lane, then a small field of wheat before they returned to the start. It was described as 'a pretty finish, seldom attained in a steeplechase, good enough for a two-year-old course.' The grandstand was in the fallow field and gave spectators a good view of every obstacle except the lane fence.

The big race at the meeting in **1859** was the Berks Open Steeplechase, over 3 miles, described as 'a miniature Grand National' and won by the unfancied *Tamworth*, carrying only 8st 12 lbs. There was an incident involving *Creeping Jane*, first in the Berks Hunt Stakes. The owner of runner-up *Anonymous* alleged that Best, the rider of the winner, was not properly qualified as he had ridden for hire in public steeplechases. The stewards turned down the objection.

The regulars at the George Hotel in Reading town centre organised a sweep in **1860** on the Berkshire Open Steeplechase on Thursday 12 January. A notebook, found soon after World War II, listed those entering and the horses they had drawn. Tickets were two shillings each, the winner receiving £1 and the runner-up ten shillings. The remaining 11 shillings 'to be spent among the subscribers in a glass of grog each'. The winner was by coincidence a Mr Chinnock, who drew *Omar Pasha* in the sweep. Could he have been the horse-dealer whose Vastern Lane premises were quite close to the George?

Whitley

After a gap of six years the Steeplechases were revived in **1866** at Mr Young's Whitley Park farm, situated to the south of what is now Cintra Park. The stewards included the Earl of Coventry, Lord Parker and the Mayor of Reading. Clerk of the course, judge and handicapper was J F Verrall, starter R Lovegrove and secretary R Tompkins.

The most exciting race proved to be the two and a half mile handicap in which Ben Land, leading on *Serious Case*, came to grief at the third from home. He caught his horse, remounted, just failed to catch the winner *Arlescott* and received a tremendous round of applause from the grandstand when he went to weigh in.

Land was not so popular at nearby Windsor, however, when he caused embarrassment to Queen Victoria in a steeplechase.

Her Majesty was watching a race from her carriage close to a fence when, Land, unaware of the Queen's presence, urged his horse to the obstacle 'in his loudest voice, with some of the choicest expressions of which he was so great a master.' The Queen, definitely not amused, left immediately. Land's father, also Ben, was a rough and ready character, a heavy gambler and a leading trainer and handler of dual Grand National victor *The Lamb.*

He had several winners at Reading Steeplechases, mostly ridden by his son, but by 1872 Land's fortunes had changed dramatically. *The Lamb* was transferred to a German owner, then Land had a bad run at the gambling tables which led to him committing suicide by slitting his jugular vein with a cut-throat razor. Ironically a month later *The Lamb* had to be destroyed after falling at Baden-Baden.

The two-day Reading Steeplechases of January **1868** were delayed for a week because of frost and snow. Racegoers from London had been keen supporters of the event, but this time there were few present. The course was in reasonable condition but the fences were a severe test for both horse and jockey, and on the second day *Cripple* and *Farnborough* both fell in the Berkshire Open Chase and had to be put down. The deaths prompted a letter from 'Castigator' to the local press:

> At the recent Reading Steeplechases, two fine horses were sacrificed, by being urged to perform jumps (under the circumstances) far beyond their physical animal power. Every frequenter of Whitley Park Farm is fully aware that in the arable portion, there is not a heavier bit of land between the Kennet and Loddon in any season. What must it have been on January 14 and 15 of this year? It is quite time that the arm of the Legislature should be directed to stop at once the ruthless sacrifice of that noble animal, the horse, (given to ungrateful man for the most beneficial purposes) and which, instead of protection, meets with a cruel and lingering death, at the hands of individuals who, for the sake of a few pounds, set animal suffering at nought, and disgrace the age they live in.

Man of all talents: Arthur Yates – jockey, owner and trainer

There was also controversy in the handicap plate on the first day. Corslett, rider of *Love In A Mist* second to *Pakington,* objected to the winner for having gone the wrong side of a flag near the farmhouse. The stewards visited the spot where *Pakington* was alleged to have run out and they found tracks on the outside of the flag as indicated by Corslett. He was awarded the race after several spectators gave evidence.

The chequered career of the Reading Steeplechases continued when they were revived in January 1872 after a gap of four years. But the local press commented scathingly about local support:

> the inhabitants of the Berkshire capital generally are as apathetic to the steeple-chases as they are to flat-racing and the immense attendance on the course included comparatively few of the town's residents. But the London division of professionals mustered in rare force, and a capital day's sport was provided.

Before the selling race Mr Ellison, who had won the opener with *Rattlesnake,* purchased *Devizes* for £30 with the promise of a 'pony' (£25) if he won. Unfortunately the horse, when going well three fences from home, broke its back. Ellison had also backed his new purchase for a sizeable stake and so finished the transaction well down, getting just £1 from the sale of the unfortunate animal's carcase.

The Morning Post correspondent echoed the thoughts four years previously of 'Castigator':

> We have little sympathy with those who are continually calling out for big and dangerous fences in steeplechasing, and the water need not be three or four feet to make horses jump. Especially is this kind of jump to be deprecated when such reckless foolhardiness and absolute cruelty is to be witnessed as that evinced by the rider of *Balsamo* in the Selling Stakes. The horse was dead beaten, and at least 50 yards behind *Miss Brunel* and *Bretby*, so that it was sheer ruffianism to 'ram' him at the last fence, the brook. The rider escaped a ducking, but *Balsamo* dislocated his shoulder and was led hobbling up the course.

There was also a two-day meeting in April, at which popular owner-trainer-rider Arthur Yates lifted the Open Hunter Stakes by a short head on 5-1 on hotshot *Crawler*, a winner of nearly 50 races for his owner in a long career. That year Yates headed the list of gentleman riders with 67 winners. He went on to train three Grand National winners – *Roquefort* (1885), *Gamecock* (1887) and *Cloister* (1893) – but did not wish to be considered a professional trainer, so the credit for the victories went to John Swatton, head lad at his Bishop's Sutton headquarters in Hampshire. In an illustrious career, Yates rode 460 horses to victory and also trained 2,950 winners. He achieved a National Hunt record of saddling five victorious horses in one afternoon at Torquay in 1905 – a mark held with several others until eclipsed in modern times by Paul Nicholls with six at Wincanton.

At the same meeting Mr W H Johnstone completed the remarkable feat of riding his horse *Chance* to victory three times – twice on the same day. He won the Scurray Handicap on the Tuesday, and was successful in the opening and last contests on the Wednesday – the two-mile Downshire Plate and a Selling Stakes.

In **1873**, two days of jump racing attracted a crowd of around 3,000 with very few of the 'rough' element and the bogus racecard gentlemen. The latter were driven away because clerk of the course Robert Tompkins, the local auctioneer based in Friar Street, arranged for racecards to be sold only by officially-appointed sellers.

The three-day Reading Steeplechases meeting in **1875** proved to be the last at Whitley. On the first day the Whitley Handicap resulted in a dead heat between *Harvester* and *Lopez*. Subsequently Mr Barnes, *Harvester*'s jockey, injured his hand while riding in the Downshire Handicap, so owner Arthur Yates steered his horse to victory in the deciding heat. *Harvester* had pulled off a great win four years earlier by emerging victorious in the Great Metropolitan Steeplechase at Croydon, beating 13 rivals. Yates maintained that his horse would have carried off the Grand National the following year but for over-reaching badly at the last Aintree fence. In the final race of the meeting, *Outpost* won the Steward's Handicap Plate – finishing alone. It was recompense for his owner Captain Whyte, who had seen his horse disqualified for interference in the Downshire Handicap on the first day.

Maiden Erlegh

On 18 May **1886** Maiden Erlegh races were held for the first time under Grand National Hunt Rules, but then they were still known as the Royal Berks Yeomanry Steeplechases. The nearly circular course was held on the eastern side of the estate of John Hargreaves, for many years master of the South Berks Hunt, whose ancestor James, in the 1760s, had invented the spinning jenny, the machine which revolutionised the cotton industry. The course extended over the area now covered by Hillside Road, Sutcliffe Avenue and Mill Lane. The grandstand stood on an area behind the houses now in Hillside Road opposite Loddon Junior School. The main gate was close to a present-day newsagents in Wokingham Road.

In the hope of excluding the 'rougher element' an entrance fee was charged, nevertheless several of the 'lower classes' from London and other towns made up the 3,000 crowd. But the presence of 40 police officers kept problems to a minimum.

A match between Mr C E Pigott's *Pleasure Boat* and Mr R S Apthorp's *Wild Norah* opened the six-race programme. It was won by *Pleasure Boat*, ridden by its owner, after *Wild Norah* fell at the open ditch. Pigott also came first on the same horse later in the fifth race, the Regimental Welter Steeplechase. The last race, the Maiden Erlegh Open Steeplechase Sweepstakes, proved the most exciting event of the day. A closely-fought affair ended with victory for the favourite *Dressmaker* by two lengths from *Zulu Chief*.

A separate annual event around this time was the point-to-point race for a cup given by John Hargreaves of Maiden Erlegh. In **1887** it was held over a course of five miles of stiff hunting country with a lot of fences and ploughed land. The 17 runners started from Swallowfield at 3pm, and when they came in view of the crowd at the Loddon Bridge finishing line Mr Allfrey on *Shamrock* led the way but fell jumping the last lane, and Mr Hargreaves junior on *Surprise* went on to win by 15 lengths. At least 150 carriages and many people on horseback had gathered at the finish together with the general public. After the main event, two individuals organised a pony race – and to the delight of the crowd one of the riders fell in the brook.

The same year Mr Stallworthy, steward to the Maiden Erlegh estate, had laid out a sporty course which included some stiff fences for the National Hunt meeting. Mr Roake, chief huntsman of the South Berks Hunt, and his men kept the course clear, and there were no serious accidents. Pigott once again completed a double, this time on *Playlight*, evens favourite for both races, even though he received a 7 lb penalty for winning the first event. John Hargreaves junior, winner of the point-to-point earlier in the year, also rode *Surprise* to victory in the United Hunt Steeplechase. The previous day he had piloted it to success at the Aldershot Divisional Steeplechases.

Several cases of 'welshing' were reported. Musical entertainment was provided by the 1st Volunteer Battalion of the Royal Berks Regiment under the direction of Bandmaster Roberts. There was an unhappy end to the day for a party of racegoers. W H Johnstone,

Official Programme—Price Sixpence.

South Berks Hunt & Royal Berks Yeomanry Cavalry

STEEPLE CHASES

AT

MAIDEN ERLEGH

(By kind permission of MAJOR HARGREAVES),

On TUESDAY, MARCH 27th, 1888,

Under Grand National Rules.

Stewards:

Colonel Willes
Major the Hon. O. Craven
Major Hargreaves
Major Allfrey
Major Thoyts
Major Ricardo
Mr. R. T. Hermon-Hodge, M.P.
Mr. H. J. Simonds
Mr. C. E. Pigott
Mr. J. Hargreaves, Jun.
Mr. E. H. Benzon
Mr. E. P. Crowdy
Mr. T. M. Eyston
Mr. W. G. Flanagan
Sergeant G. Ayres

Judge—COL. WILLES. *Starter*—MAJOR RICARDO.
Clerk of the Course and Scales and Auctioneer—Mr. H. A. STEVENS.
Hon. Sec. and Stakeholder—Mr. H. J. BEARD.

Admission to Course, 1s. Stand & Paddock, 5s.

GOOD ACCOMMODATION WILL BE PROVIDED FOR HORSES.

No one allowed on the ground till after 12 o'clock, and no Carriages allowed on the Course without payment of the following charges:—

Brakes, £1 1s.; 4-wheel Carriage, 15s.; 2-wheel ditto, 5s.

No Vans, Waggons, Carts, Saddle Horses, or Dogs allowed.

BRADLEY AND SON, PRINTERS, READING.

Programme: Maiden Erlegh Steeplechases, 1888

Politician: R T Hermon-Hodge, MP for Accrington, steward at Maiden Erlegh

accompanied by two ladies, was driving into Reading in an open carriage when he collided with another vehicle near the Three Tuns at Earley. It overturned and the passengers were thrown out. Johnstone suffered a broken leg, and the driver a bad head wound, but luckily the ladies escaped injury.

The meeting continued to gather momentum, and in **1888** the official programme (price sixpence) stated that admission to the course was one shilling, while the stand and paddock was five shillings. No-one was allowed in the ground until 12 noon, neither were carriages permitted on the course until payment of the following charges: brakes £1.1s; four-wheel carriages 15s; two-wheel carriages 5s. No vans, wagons, carts, saddle horses or dogs allowed. Among the stewards for the meeting was local resident Robert Trotter Hermon-Hodge, MP for Accrington, a politician deemed worthy of a 'Spy' cartoon in the weekly magazine Vanity Fair. One of his claims to fame was that while at Oxford University he grew a very long moustache, which he maintained throughout his political career.

An estimated 2,500 spectators paid for admission in **1889**. No fewer than 50 policemen, plus detectives, were present to maintain good order. The well-behaved crowd were entertained during the afternoon by the Reading Town Band. The only real incident involved Mr F Headington's *Prince Herbert* in the Sellers' Hunters' Steeplechase. Towards the finish, a man ran across the course and was sent spinning by the horse; luckily he only suffered bruises. The famous amateur jockey Captain Roddy Owen, an officer in the Lancashire Fusiliers, rode *Silver Star* and *Cabin Boy* to victory to repeat his double of the previous year.

Because the **1891** meeting took place in the week after Easter, attendance of the 'working classes' was below average, but this was offset by large numbers of the county gentry. It was reported there was 'no rowdyism, welshing or pocket-picking' thanks mainly to the usual large presence of Berks police. There was also a posse of detectives from London. For the first time a Stewards' Enclosure for carriages was fenced off opposite the Grandstand. It was hoped to repeat the experiment the following year, with perhaps an improvement in the temporary railings.

Roddy Owen rode the last of his five winners at Maiden Erlegh when he piloted *Edio* to victory. The next year he won the Grand National on *Father O'Flynn*, his final race in England. Two days later Owen applied for foreign service with his regiment, and in 1896 died of cholera in Egypt during the Dongola expedition. Sir J Rendell Rodd, in his book 'Social and Diplomatic Memories', describes Owen as 'a consummate horseman and knight errant of adventure'.

Owen's mount *Edio*, a 9-4 on chance, was owned by 'Mr Abington', the racing alias of the young Scottish millionaire George Alexander Baird, who also met an untimely end. He had inherited a fortune from his father, a Glasgow iron-founder, and died in 1893 in his early thirties. After a life spent in the wrong company, he ended up an alcoholic. He was a friend of Lillie Langtry, former mistress of the Prince of Wales. Baird had won the 1887 Derby with *Merry Hampton*.

Hulton Archive/Getty Images

Hero: Roddy Owen, army officer and gentleman jockey

In **1892** there were 60 entries for the six races, but the eventual fields proved to be very small. Four of the events were won by short-priced favourites, and the Selling Steeplechase was declared void, as none of the four runners could be induced to negotiate the course.

Beautiful spring weather attracted a record crowd to the races in **1893**. McKie, rider of *Haggis*, the favourite for the Maiden Erlegh Steeplechase Plate, broke his collar-bone when his horse fell.

By good fortune Mr Walker, a surgeon, happened to be nearby at the time and attended to the fracture. An added attraction for racegoers was the presence of royalty. HRH Prince Christian travelled from his Windsor home, Cumberland Lodge, to lunch at Maiden Erlegh, along with the Duchess of Wellington and the Marquis of Downshire, as guests of John Hargreaves. To round off a full day the Prince left to dine with the Prince of Wales at Marlborough House, London, in the evening.

Prince Christian, a keen sportsman and son-in-law of Queen Victoria, repeated his visit in **1894** and dined with the Hargreaveses again. He was a keen follower of the Garth Hounds, a local hunt, and enjoyed shooting parties. It was said that the walls of his home were decked with hunting trophies. Unfortunately the latter pursuit led to injury when his brother-in-law, the Duke of Connaught, took a bad aim and shot out the Prince's left eye. There was an even more serious equine accident at Maiden Erlegh on the day of the Prince's visit when *Edward,* owned by Mrs H W Benyon, suffered a broken back at the second brook and had to be shot.

Very heavy rainstorms kept the attendance down at the **1895** Wednesday meeting. W C Keeping, owner of *Ancho, Greenhill* and *Biscuit,* took three of the six races – the Reading Steeplechase Handicap Plate, Selling Steeplechase Plate and the United Hunt Steeplechase Plate, total value £190. *Biscuit* had completed a treble, after winning the previous two years at Maiden Erlegh. The mare went on to come third behind *The Soarer* in the Grand National at Aintree the following year after leading with two fences to go.

Although John Hargreaves had passed away since the last meeting, the **1896** races went ahead by permission of his executors, and sunny weather attracted another record attendance. Remarkably, half the 32 runners fell, but there were no serious injuries to horses or riders. There was controversy in the Maiden Erlegh Steeplechase Plate: the winner, *Olive Branch,* was disqualified for taking the wrong course and the race was awarded to *Sting,* who finished second. Mr E P Gundry, owner of *Olive Branch,* asked permission to appeal to the National Hunt Committee, but the local stewards refused his request.

It was a fine spring day for the **1897** meeting, but a fresh wind blew dust about to make life far from pleasant for carriage

Walkover: *I.O.U* had no opposition in the 1897 Maiden Erlegh Steeplechase

people and pedestrians. The card was competitive, except for the Maiden Erlegh Steeplechase over two miles, in which *I.O.U.* walked over.

Bad weather marred the next two years' meetings. In **1898**, a strong wind got up during the course of the afternoon and blew down the horse tent, leaving the animals shivering in the cold.

The **1899** races were put back for a week because of frozen snow on the course. The Tradesmen's Steeplechase Plate attracted only one entry. The Reading tradesmen had subscribed 40 sovereigns to the race, so Mr E H Polehampton's *Sting* walked over for a prize of £20. The Reading Steeplechase went to Mr H E Elwes's *Corabie*, who had won the previous day at Sir Robert Wilmot's Hawthorn Hill meeting.

In **1900** the new century marked the first meeting under the patronage of Sol Joel, the diamond magnate, who was a millionaire by the time he was 20. He had obtained a lease of Maiden Erlegh, was chairman of the executive and introduced many improvements to the rings and paddocks. Joel was so pleased with the day's racing that he intended to apply for a licence for a two-day meeting the next Spring. A highlight of the afternoon was the extra event added to the six-race programme. It was a match between

Mr H Caversham Simonds's *Horoscope* and Oliver Dixon's *No Name.* Dixon's led for two-thirds of the two-mile hurdle race, but *Horoscope* rushed to the front and prevailed by four lengths.

The first two-day meeting of **1901** was hit by miserable conditions, with a biting north-easterly wind and frequent rain

Ace of Diamonds: Sol Joel, owner of Maiden Erlegh Court

and snow showers. Sol Joel had promised that the profits from the meeting were to be given to local charitable organisations, but these were small because of the poor attendance. Joel had his first success at Maiden Erlegh when his chestnut gelding *Uncle Jack* lifted the Great Western Handicap Steeplechase over three miles. *Uncle Jack* took the lead in the three-horse race after a quarter of a mile and won easily by a distance from *Astronomy*, who was a long way in front of *Tavora*.

Sol Joel achieved a back-to-back double on the second day of the first autumn meeting at Maiden Erlegh. His chestnut horse *Sly Fox* won the Henley Selling Hurdle Handicap and was bought in for 65gns. Then his gelding *Mintstalk* lifted the Maiden Erlegh Handicap Chase, both winners being ridden by amateur jockey Frank Hartigan.

The popularity of the meeting was growing, and race day specials were run by the Great Western and London & South Western Railways. Bayles's Racecourse Atlas stated:

> This little Berkshire fixture has made rapid progress towards popularity since the place was taken over by Mr S B Joel, who proposes making many improvements in the course. It is now a nice little meeting, well patronised, with several steeplechases and hurdle races of £140 in value, including the Erlegh Cup. The minor events range from £40 to £70. The course is one and a quarter miles round, running left-handed, with a very short run-in from the last fence. It is half a mile from Maiden Erlegh Station [now Earley]. The country is rural, and somewhat hilly, but the fences are made of gorse with the exception of the brook, which is a watercourse about 350 yards past the stand at the bottom of a rather steep declivity.

Over 4,500 racegoers attended at the opening day of the **1902** Spring meeting and this was almost matched the following day. An alleged theft at the racecourse came before a special County Bench at Wokingham: George Robert Quinn, a bookmaker's clerk of no fixed abode, was charged with stealing a pair of field-glasses, the property of Frederick Woodland. He was remanded in custody. Reading jockey Matthews was successful on the second day of the November meeting when he rode

Mr F R Hunt's *Billy George* to victory in the Maiden Erlegh Handicap Chase. The most popular win in the two days was that of Major Caversham Simonds's *Gentle Hilda* in the Novices' Chase.

Joel had now purchased Maiden Erlegh and made improvements to the course costing £2,000 in time for the two-day November meeting in **1903**. The paddock had been doubled in size, and new brick buildings were erected to provide a press room, weighing room, stewards' room and another for the remaining officials. There was a well-staffed telegraph office, and a new stand in the cheap enclosure had an excellent view of the course. The reserved lawn was unchanged, but there were considerable improvements to the private enclosure and Mr Joel's stand, while new number boards were put up.

At the same time Joel was making alterations to his new home. He added a marble palm court to be used as a winter garden, looking onto superb gardens. Joel was also fond of statues, which featured inside and outside the main building. He gave tremendous parties and would have as many as 200 guests at his 'Sunday before Ascot luncheons'. There were also 39 bedroom suites, three reception rooms and many bathrooms. But the pièce de resistance was a marble heated indoor swimming pool, 64 feet long. He liked to have London show-girls in attendance to entertain his guests. A group of these ladies were invited to have a swim but had no costumes. Joel produced some which, he claimed, were made of a special new waterproof material. However, much to the amusement of the male guests the swimsuits disintegrated on contact with the water. Apart from his ostentatious side, Joel was of a generous nature and many organisations in the town of Reading benefited immensely, including Reading University, the Royal Berkshire Hospital and Reading Football Club. He also gave £10,000 to the National Playing Fields Association and provided the Sol Joel recreation ground, opened by the Duke of York in 1927.

The Wednesday of the Spring meeting in **1904** was notable for the adventures of *Blue Knight* during and after the 2.15 Twyford Selling Steeplechase Handicap. The horse, trained by J E P Rogers of Cheltenham, fell on the second circuit, unseating its rider. It continued along the course to the paddock, rushed round the

Top man: William Dollery, Grand National winner and successful at Reading

enclosure and jumped a high spiked iron fence behind the grandstand into the park. Then it raced across the park, leapt over oak palings into the Wokingham Road, knocked down a policeman and dashed along the main road. Opposite the Three Tuns Alfred Dell, a labourer of Abbey Street, tried to stop the runaway horse but was knocked down. The constable was not hurt, and miraculously Dell suffered only minor injuries. The animal carried on past the tram terminus at the junction with St Peter's Road and, though frightened, instinctively found its way back to Dixon's yard and stables in Crescent Road, where it had arrived from Cheltenham the same morning.

Oliver Dixon, a great supporter of racing at Maiden Erlegh, was also one of the best-known horse-dealers in the country; he sold horses to most of the top stables in Britain and Europe. His clients included King George V and other royalty. Dixon died in 1939 at the age of 69, the day after watching two of his horses win at the Aldershot Military Meeting.

This year a fifth day's racing was introduced in late April, and was the only Saturday meeting in the history of Maiden

Clearing the Stand fence: Maiden Erlegh Steeplechase, 1905

Erlegh. It was not a success, as only 27 horses took part in the seven races.

The two-day November meeting was marred by bitterly cold conditions, and on the opening day snow fell until midday, but the weather improved on the next day as did the crowds, swelled by 'many sportsmen having journeyed from Warwick.'

On the first day an interesting runner was 6-1 chance *Matchboard* in the Theale Selling Hurdle. The four-year-old was owned jointly by Charlie Wood, a retired jockey of some repute turned trainer, and theatrical agent Max Barthropp, who surprised everyone by wanting to ride his own horse. *Matchboard* edged out *Away West*, ridden by Grand National-winning jockey William Dollery, by a neck. The winner was sold to Mr F R Hunt for 50 guineas.

GREAT WESTERN RAILWAY.

Maiden Erlegh Steeplechases,

WEDNESDAY and THURSDAY,

November 15th & 16th, 1905.

ON THE ABOVE DATES

Cheap Tickets

WILL BE ISSUED TO

READING

From	By Trains as under.		Return Fares. 1st Class.	2nd Class.	3rd Class.
	A.M.	A.M.	s. d.	s. d.	s. d.
Swindon ...	9 15	10 50	8 9	5 5	4 4
		NOON			
Shrivenham ...	9 25	12 0	7 6	4 9	3 9
Faringdon ...	9 22	12 0	7 3	4 7	3 8
Uffington ...	9 38	12 13	6 3	4 1	3 3
Challow ...	9 46	12 21	5 10	3 9	2 11
Wantage Road	9 56	12 31	5 6	3 2	2 7
Steventon ...	10 8	12 42	4 5	2 9	2 2
		A.M.			
Oxford ...	9 35	11 35	5 8	3 9	2 11
Abingdon ...	9 30	11 12	5 3	3 4	2 8
Radley ...	9 46	11 46	4 9	3 2	2 5

From	By Trains as under.		Return Fares. 1st Class.	2nd Class.	3rd Class.
	A.M.	NOON	s. d.	s. d.	s. d.
Culham ...	9 53	11 53	4 2	2 8	2 1
Didcot	10 24	12 5	3 7	2 4	1 10
Wallingford ...	10 20	12 2	3 2	2 0	1 7
Cholsy & Moulsf'd	10 34	12 16	2 6	1 8	1 4
Goring & Streatley	10 43	12 26	1 11	1 3	1 0
Newbury ...	10 33	11 39	3 7	2 4	1 10
Thatcham ...	9 25	11 57	2 10	1 10	1 5
Midgham ...	9 31	12 3	2 3	1 6	1 2
Aldermaston ...	9 37	12 9	1 11	1 3	1 0
Basingstoke ...	10 5	11 45	3 2	2 1	1 8
Bramley ...	10 15	11 56	2 3	1 6	1 2
Mortimer ...	10 23	12 3	1 6	1 2	1 0

The Tickets will be available for return from Reading by any train after 4.0 p.m. on the day of issue only

Children under Three years of age, Free; Three and under Twelve, Half-Price.

THE TICKETS ARE NOT TRANSFERABLE.

NO LUGGAGE ALLOWED.

Should an Excursion or Cheap Ticket be used for any other Station than those named upon it, or by any other Train than as above specified, it will be rendered void, and therefore the Fare paid will be liable to forfeiture, and the full Ordinary Fare will become chargeable.

PADDINGTON, November, 1905. **JAMES C. INGLIS, General Manager.**

L.D. 277. 1,000. R.D. 300. Wyman & Sons, Ltd., Printers, Fetter Lane, London, E.C., and Reading.—2274a.

Away Day: Excursion bill for Maiden Erlegh Steeplechases, 1905

There were a few spills during the meeting, but the riders escaped serious hurt, the worst being that sustained by R Woodland on the opening day. He experienced a nasty fall at the preliminary obstacle in the Juvenile Hurdle race, his jaw dislocated through a kick in the face. Medical attention at the course appeared to be first-class, and Dr Heasman, quickly in attendance, set the jaw and attended to the rider's other injuries. In the first race, a Maiden Hurdle, Jack Joel (Sol's brother) was successful with *His Lordship,* who beat Mr Harold Lawrence's *Llanstephan* into second spot. In his biography 'Racing Reminiscences' Tom Rees, trainer of *Llanstephan,* recalled that he did not wish to run the horse, but his owner insisted. Jack Joel was really impressed by the performance of the three-year-old, as *His Lordship* had won the Wokingham Stakes in 1902. Rees said: 'Mr Joel offered Mr Lawrence £1,000 for *Llanstephan,* which I regret to say was refused. The race practically finished his career.'

Freezing weather for the November **1905** meeting kept the crowds down, and entries were small. There was rain, hail and snow on the opening day, and while conditions improved the following afternoon it was still heavy going and overcast. Perhaps the low turnout of public and horses led Joel to have second thoughts about continuing the meeting.

The last Maiden Erlegh races were held on Wednesday and Thursday 11 and 12 April **1906**. The officials were: Stewards: Mr S B Joel, Sir Robert Wilmot Bart, Major H Caversham Simonds, Mr Arthur Yates and Mr E Bird. Secretary: Mr M Ackett. Starter: Mr H Redford. Stakeholder: Mr T Honey. Clerk of the Scales: Mr A P I'Anson. Handicapper: Mr A Keyser. Auctioneer: Mr H A Stevens. Judge: Mr A S Manning. Clerk of the Course: Mr W E Bushby.

Unfortunately the going was on the hard side, and several horses which had travelled to Earley did not run. On the first day only 23 horses competed in the six events, and three of these were matches. However it provided a hat-trick of victories for 25-year-old trainer Frank Hartigan from three runners. Hartigan, son of an army veterinary officer, subsequently had major triumphs on the jumps and flat. He trained the 1930 Grand National victor *Shaun Goilin* and two classic-winning fillies, *Vaucluse* and *Roseway*, successful in the 1,000 Guineas of 1915 and 1919. On the second day the last ever winner at the course was the favourite *Sonning*, ridden by William Rollison, in the Great Western Handicap Steeplechase over three miles and 130 yards.

Sol Joel wanted to develop Maiden Erlegh as a stud farm, so the victory of *Sonning*, named after the Thames-side village a couple of miles away, appropriately brought an end to racing under Rules in the Reading area.

On the flat racing scene, the year of 1906 proved to be a golden one for Sol Joel. A couple of months after that final meeting at Maiden Erlegh, he won the Ascot Gold Cup with *Batchelor's Button*, who broke the hearts of the nation by beating the well-loved *Pretty Polly*. Then in the autumn Joel lifted the Cambridgeshire Handicap with *Polymelus*, who went on to become an outstanding success at the new Maiden Erlegh stud. He was a champion sire

Appendix A: Bulmershe Heath winners

b = bay; bl = black; br = brown; c = colt; ch = chestnut;
f = filly; g = gelding; g or gr = grey; h= horse; m = mare

1727 Mr Heathcote's b g *Plain Dealer*
Sir Tho Reynell's sorrell h *Merry Batchelor*
Mr Buckworth's g g *Wanton Willy*

1728 Mr Eastwick's b g *Traveller*
Mr Packer's gr m *Berkshire Lady*
Mr Hollier's g h *Tippling John*

1729 Mr Peck's b m *Fair Rosamund*
Mr Peck's ch h *Jack-a-dandy*
Mr Maggot's ch m *Creeping-Molly*

1730 Mr Greenwood's gr h *Grey Crabb*
Mr Lee's b g *Young Captain*
Mr Adams's *Finebones*

1731 Mr Vaughan's bl h *Crutches*
Sir Henry Inglefield's b g *Marlington*
Mr Boot's br g *Ruff-Country-Dick*

1732 Earl of Portmore's b h *Merry Andrew*

1733 Mr Howes's bl h *Stilts*
Mr Trecle's bl m *Bonny-Black*
Mr Riley's b m *Bonny-Kate*

1734 Mr Seaman's g g *Foxhunter*
Mr Goodwin's b m
Mr Hobson's *Snip*

1735 No racing recorded

1736 Lord Weymouth's ch h *Flush*
Mr Trekell's b m *Rat*
Mr Thornton's g g *Caps*

1737 Mr Cook's sorrel g *Steel*
Mr Bambridge's b g *Red-Rose*

1738 Mr Marshall's b h *Benny-Batchelor*
Mr Pitt's b m *Little-Gift*
Mr Coles's br m *Pretty Polly*

1739 Mr Bevor's ch h *Driver*
Mr Sirrett's b m *Miss Read*
Mr Bingham's g g *Harlequin*

1740 Mr Harpur's b h *Blaze*
Mr Larking's gr h *Loeby*
Mr Dodd's b m *Blowsy-Bella*
Mr St John's ch h *Foxhunter*
Mr Becher's ch h *Gay*
M Whitlock's br g *Foxhunter*

1741 Mr St John's ch h *Foxhunter*
Mr Panton's b m *Diana*
Mr Figg's b m *Dairy Maid*

1742 Mr Grisewood's ch h *Careless*
Mr Corker's ch h *Watch them and catch them*
Mr Gill's g h *Hack*

1743 Mr Martindale's gr h *Starling*
Sir Humphrey Monoux's ch h *Fitzwilliams*
Mr Grisewood's gr h *Partner*

1744 Lord Wm Manners's bl h *Black Jack*
Mr Seawell's b g *Fanny's Grig*
Duke of Beaufort's b h *Punch*

1745 Mr Seddon's b h *Poppet*
Mr Robinson Lytton's g h *Cub*
Earl of Portmore's g h *Trip*

1746 Lord Leigh's ch h *Saucebox*
Mr Jenning's sorrel g *Conqueror*
Mr Parson's *Babraham*

1747 Mr Grevill's b h *Sultan*
Mr Poulet's b m *Sweetest When Naked*
Mr Grevill's b h *Sultan*

1748 Capt Becher's br g *Wheel to the Right*
Mr Paunceford's b g *Prince Charles*
Mr Canning's b m *Smiling Molly*

1749 Mr Grisewood's br m *Phoebe*
Mr Jennison's g g *Favourite*
Hon Miss Leigh's br m *Diana*

1750 Mr Carver's b h *Whitefoot*
Mr Swymmer's ch g
Mr Marshall's ch h *Little Driver*

1751 Lord Onslow's br g *Highlander*
Mr Churchill's b g *What You Please*
Mr Marshall's ch h *Little Driver*

1752 Mr Lake's ch g *Farmer*
Capt Clarke's ch h *Running Trooper*

1753 Lord Byron's ch h *Lightening*
Mr Fettyplace's b g *Babraham*
Lord Chedworth's ch h *Poor Robin*

1754 Mr Lamego's ch h *Little Driver*
Mr Fettyplace's b m *Molly of the Vale*
Mr Rogers's ch g *Hay-Over*

1755 Lord Onslow's g h *Martin*
Mr Swymmer's bl g *Wart*
Mr Chamberlane's b h *Ruby*

1756 Mr Brooks's b m *Lady-Thigh*
Dr Hayes's *Staghunter*
Mr Deane's *Partner*
Mr Bowls's *Milo*

1757 Mr Pitt's b h *Liberty*
Mr Churchill's b g *Slider*

1758 Mr Swymmer's b h *Tantivie*
Lord Thanet's b g *Thrift*

1759 Lord Chedworth's b h *Babram*
Mr Osbaldeston's b g *Sportsman*
Mr Rogers's ch m *Fair Rachael*

1760 Mr Sparrow's b h
Mr Benwell's gr g
Mr Rogers's ch m *Fair Rachael*

1761 Sir J Dashwood's b h *Ramper*
Lord Craven's ch h *Foxhunter*
Mr Hilliars's ch m *Fair Rachael*

1762 Mr Stroud's gr h (late *Prospect*)
Mr Withers' gr m *Lincolnshire Lady*
Mr Hilliar's b m *Violet*

1763 Mr Wildman's b h
Mr Wilson's b h
Lord Castlehaven's ch m *Milk Maid*

1764 Mr Rickett's ch h
Mr Green's gr c *Gimcrack*
Mr Marshall's b m *Diana*

1765 Mr Humphrey's b h *Trifle*
Lord Corysford's b f
Mr Quick's b h *Stranger*

1766 Mr Brown's g g *Ploughboy*
Mr Stroud's g f *Tinetta*
Mr Quick's b h *Stranger*

1767 Mr Gibbons's b m *Dorothy*
Mr King's g f
Mr Castle's b h *Stranger*

1768 Mr Smith's b h *Brutus*
Mr Warrington's gr c *Young Gimcrack*
Sir Frederick Evelyn's gr g *Badger*

1769 Mr Strode's b h *Foxhunter*
Mr Carver's ch h *Pincher*
Sir Fredreick Evelyn's gr g *Badger*

1770 Capt O'Kelly's ch m *Davy-maid*

1771 Capt O'Kelly's b h *Rumble*
Capt Stroude's br f *Almira*
Capt Stroude's br h *Little Joe*

1772 Mr Cope's b g *Prussia*
Mr Bishop's ch h *Cicero*
Mr Salt's b c *Nestor*

1773 Duke of Grafton's br m *Promise*
Mr Barley's ch h *Venom*
Duke of Bolton's b c *Chose*

1774 Mr Burlton's b h *Cyrus*
Mr Belson's dun h *Don Dun*
Mr Dymock's ch c *Sparkler*

1775 Mr Yates's b g *Wafer*
Duke of Bolton's b h *Tidedol*
Mr Compton's b f *Hemel*

1776 Sir John Shelly's br h *Ovid*
Mr Neville's b c by *Chrysolite*
Lady Bampfield's b h *Bauble*

1777 Lord Craven's b h *King Hiram*
Mr Moody's b h *Furiband*
Mr Stamford's ch f *Betty*

1778 Mr Dymock's ch h *Lucullus*
Mr Gosling's ch m *Betty*
Duke of Bolton's f *Cow*

1779 Mr Shorter's b m *Leonara*
Mr Rider's ch h *Defence*
Mr Goodison's ch c *Xillo-aloe*

1780 Mr Broadhurst's br h *Pompey*
Mr Parker's c f *Luna*
Mr Parker's f by *Prophet*
Mr Bullock's b f
Mr Parker's f by *Pistol*

1781 Capt Bertie's br h *Flying Jib*
Mr Tate's b m *Miss Nightingale*
Capt Bertie's b c *Jocunda*

1782 Mr Freeman's ch h *Standby*
Mr Bertie's *Shag* by Marsk out of *Tuzzimuzzy*
Capt Hoar's b h *Copper Bottom*
Mr Carter's b c

1783 Mr Compton's br h *Cottager*
Mr Watts's gr h *Medley*
Mr Adams's gr c *Puff*

1784 Mr Wynch's b h *Little John*
Sir Frederick Evelyn's b c

1785 Mr Panton's b c *Pindar*
Duke of Queensberry's b c *Arrow*
Sir Frederick Evelyn's ch h *Gallant*

1786 Mr Watts's b m *Miss Kingsland*
Mr Hilton's dun m *Miss Tiffany*
Mr Lade's gr c *Pilot*
Mr Lade's br f *Letitia*

1787 Mr Belson's c c *Prodigal*
Mr Lade's gr c *Pilot*
Mr Rogers's br f *Pumpkin*

1788 Mr Rogers's b f *Seedling*
Mr Rogers's b c *Buffer*
Sir F Evelyn's ch f *Mira*

1789 Mr Clark's ch c *Troy*
Mr Churchill's b m *Star*
Mr Pickering's br g *Clodhopper*
Mr Lade's *Plutitia*
Mr Clark's *Schoolboy*
Mr Leeson's br h *Curricle*
Mr Whitburn's br c by *Highflyer*
Mr Nottage's h *Oak Apple*
Mr Powney's m *Romp*

1790 Lord Barrymore's gr h *Highlander*
Mr Ximenes's ch m *Coquette* – walkover
Lord Barrymore's gr h *Highlander*
Mr Hamond's *Blackcock*
Mr Barry's b g *Everlasting*
Mr Hamond's bl h *Minos*
Lord Barrymore's gr h by *Magog*
Lord Barrymore's roan f *Skewball*
Mr Davis's gr c *Pallafox*
Mr Perren's ch g *Tongs*

1791 Mr Hamond's g h *Highlander*
Lord Falkland's brother to *Phaeton* – walkover
Lord Barrymore's *Halbert*
Mr Hamond's *Minos*

1792 Mr Lade's *Pantaloon*
Mr Parker's *Ensign*

1793 Mr Richardson's *Thalia*
Mr Parker's *Crab*
Lord Belfast's *Forester*
Mr Haggard's b c

1794 Mr Annesley's *No Pretender*
Mr Annesley's *Pandolpho*
Mr Durant's b f

1795 Mr Annesley's *Pandolpho*
Mr Clarke's *Victor*
Lord Egremont's b f by *Mercury*

1796 Mr Stapleton's b f *Susannah*
Mr Stapleton's b f *Susannah*

1797 Mr Dolphin's b h *Rowland*
Mr Durand's *Whip*

1798 Mr Lade's g h *Will*
Sir T Wallace's b c *Heart of Oak*

1799 Lord Sackville's *Heart of Oak*
Mr Lade's *Truss*
Mr Durand's bl f *Princess*

1800 Mr Whalley's b c *Vivaldi*
Mr Whalley's c c *Expedition*
Mr Smith's *Goldfinch*
Hon T Coventry's ch c *Scarapant*
Mr Forth's b f *Lady Skirmish*
Capt Mabbott's b g

1801 Mr Dilly's ch c *Brighton*
Mr Frogley's g h *Ploughboy*
Mr Smith's ch g *Emperor*
Mr Sadler's b c *Phyrrus*

1802 Mr Smith's b c brother to *Chuckley*
Capt Barton's b m *Novice*
Capt Taylor's ch h *Slap Bang*
Mr Storer's ch g *Emperor*
Colonel Gower's h *Hackneyman*

1803 Col Kingscote's ch c *Woodpecker*
Mr Abbey's ch m *Margery*
Mr Ladbrook's ch m *Marianne*

1804 Mr Fenwick's *Miss Coiner*
Captain Brathwayt's *Miss Bailey*

1805 Mr Congreve's ch h *Quiz*
Lord Barrymore's b h *Merryman*
Lord Barrymore's b g *Little John*
Mr Skinner's *Duckling*

1806 Mr Bigg's br f *Margaretta*
Mr Ladbroke's *Epsom Lass*
Lord Braybrooke's *Timekeeper*
Mr Embden's *Lattitat*

1807 Mr Henry's br c *Great O*
Mr Bigg's br m *Margaretta*

1808 Lord Barrymore's *Miranda*
Mr Dilly's *Gnatho*
Mr Dilly's *Gnatho*
Lord Barrymore's *Miranda* – walkover
Lord Barrymore's *Pavilion*
Mr Sell's b m *Empress*

1809 Mr Dilly's b h *Gnatho*
Sir F Evelyn's ch h by *Gohanna*
Mr Dilly's b h *Gnatho*
Mr Craven's *Inconstant*

1810 Mr Dilly's bl h *Japan*
Mr F Craven's *Jannette*
Mr F Craven's *John-o-Gaunt*
Mr Dilly's b f *Nymphina*

1811 Mr Dundas's f *Philadelphia*
Ld C H Somerset's b h *Sunbeam*
Mr Hallett's b g *Levant*

1812 Mr Harrison's b f *Grace*
Mr Hallett's *Coeleb's*
Mr Pearce's f *Caroline*
Mr Richardson's c by *Totteridge*

1813 Mr Dundas's *Romeo* – walkover
Mr Eade's ch h *Accident*
Mr Eade's ch h *Accident*
Mr Eade's ch h *Accident*
Mr Dundas's ch c by *Meteor*
Capt Montagu's b m *Johny*
Mr Eade's ch h *Accident*

1814 Mr Batson's *Doras*
Mr Hallett's f by *Beninbrough*
Mr Brown's b f by *Orville*
Mr Prior's *Rose*

Appendix B: King's Meadow winners

Jockeys names in brackets

1843 Mr Day's *Slane* (Wakefield)
Mr Day's brother to *Marius* (Wakefield)
Mr C Batten's *Norma* – walkover
Mr Teale's *Donald Caird* (Higgins)
Mr Field's *Variety* (Parr)

1844 Mr Hepple's *Lady Flora* (Bateson)
Mr Coleman's *Devil-among-the-Tailors* (Penny)
Mr Preston's *Bosphorus* (Preston)
Mr Bladon's *Palaemon*
Mr S Scott's b g by *Defence* out of *Negress* (Abdale)
Mr England's *Springbok* (Rice)
Mr Preston's *Bosphorus* (Preston)
Mr Quinton's *Pretty Doe* (Edwards)

1845 Mr Death's *Camelia* (Hutchinson)
Mr Coleman's *Devil-among-the-Tailors* (Wakefield)
Mr Tubb's *Palaemon* (Wakefield)
Mr Cook's *Carillon* (Wakefield)
Mr S Scott's *Flat-fish* (Mann)
Mr Coleman's *Devil-among-the-Tailors* (Coleman)
Mr Tubb's *Palaemon* (Crickman)

1846 Mr P P Rolt's *Stittenham* (Lord Glamis) – walkover
Mr Osbaldeston's *Secutor* (Wakefield)
Mr Drinkald's *Mongrel* (Ford)
Mr Legh's *Correct Card* (Parson)
Mr Treen's *Wild Roe* (Wakefield)
Mr WH Fuller's *Tartar* (T Day)
Mr Death's *Camelia* (Wakefield)
Mr Osbaldeston's *Secutor* (Wakefield)
Mr Palmer's *Gaiety* (Palmer jun)

1847 Mr Stapleford's *Carissima* (H Darling)
Mr Bristow's *Marietta* (Hutchinson)
Mr G Simmond's *Urina* (Pettit)
Mr Osbaldestone's *Cerberus* (Sharpe)
Mr H Elwes's *Messenger* – walkover
Mr Drinkald's *Good Boy* (Pettit)
Mr Death's *Urania* (Wakefield)
Mr W Russell's *Campanile* (Edwards)

1848 Mr Bosley's *Conquest* (Brookes)
Lord Brownlow Cecil's *Antagonist* (Donaldson)
Mr Elwes's *Conveyancer* (Elwes)
Mr Turner's *Fox Whelp* (Wakefield)
Mr Wood's *Amazement* (Kitchener)
Mr Osbaldeston's *Fugleman* (Abdale)
Duke of Richmond's *Plough Boy* (Kitchener)
Mr Bateman's *Bacchanalian* (Kitchener)
Mr Wood's *Amazement* (Abdale)

1849 Mr Waller's *Captain Parry* (Wakefield)
Mr I Day's *Eagle's Plume* (Wakefield)
Mr Drinkald's *The Juggler* (Rodney)
Mr Waller's *Pottinger* (Wakefield)
Mr Gregory's *Skudar* (Treen)
Mr Cowley's *Second Sight* (Sabine)
Mr Greville's *Estafette* (Flatman)
Mr Southby's *The Streamer* (Wakefield jun)

1850 Lord John Scott's *Defaulter* (Abdale)
Mr Drinkald's *Dulcet* (Rodney)
Mr Jones's *Calmar* (Holdway)
Mr Osbaldeston's unnamed chestnut colt (Barker)
Lord John Scott's *Windhound* (Hiett)
Mr Southby's *Vesta* (Lowe)
Lord H Lennox's *Turtle* (Kitchener)
Mr Drinkald's *Dulcet* (Rodney)

1851 Mr Formby's *Teeswater* (R Sherwood)
Mr E Jones's *Melford* (Thick)
Mr Carew's *Shropshire Witch* (A Day)
Mr Drewe's *Batwing* (Love)
Mr Evans's *Zingaric* (Holdway)
Mr Drinkald's *Grey Tommy* (A Day)
Mr Bickham's *No Chance* (Burns)
Mr Russell's *Docility* (Thick)

1852 Mr Wortley's br g by *Idas* (Cowley)
Mr Drinkald's *Dulcet* (Pavis)
Mr G Drewe's *Defiance* (Hiett)
Mr Bingley's *Christmas* (Graybrook)
Mr Sherring's *Rage* (Steele)
Mr Harvey's *Prestige* (Wakefield)
Lord John Scott's *Pug Orrock* (Whitehouse)
Mr I Day's *Waterfall* (Wakefield) – walkover
Mr Thompson's *Blood Royal* (Hiett)
Mr Wortley's br g by *Idas* (Kendall)

1853 Mr Spencer's *Prevention* (J Goater)
Mr Drewe's *Vixen* (Kendall)
Mr Waller's *Octavia* (Crouch)
Mr G Drewe's *Shipwreck* (Kendall)
Mr Jones's *Young Cecilia* (Corderoy)
Mr H Hill's *Ireland's Eye* (A Day)
Mr Wanchope's *Calliope* (Kendall)
Mr Dilworth's *The Queen's Own* (Kendall)
Mr J Day's *Waterfall* (Wakefield)
Mr T Smith's *Epilogue* (Alder)

1854 Mr Bloss's *Herbert* (Hawkes)
Mr Saxon's *Evangeline* (Foster)
Mr Drinkald's brother to *Grey Tommy* (Wells)
Mr Fenning's *Michaelmas Maid* (Capt Lane)
Lord John Scott's *Morgan Le Faye* (Wells)
Mr Bloss's *Mirabeau* (Charlton)

Capt Berkeley's *Bright Phoebus* (Capt Berkeley)
Mr Waller's *Octavia* (Wakefield)
Lord John Scott's *Clotide* (G Whitehouse)
Mr Dray's *Little Gerard* (Wells)
Mr Hill's *Dan Cupid* (Palmer)
Mr Waller's *Octavia* (Wakefield)
Mr Land's *Dartford* (Land jnr)

1855 Mr Mellish's *Gossip* (Wells)
Mr Treen's *Imogene* (Fordham)
Mr J M Stanley's *Schamyl* (Ashmall)
Mr H Stone's *The Fair Geraldine* (Harrison)
Mr W Day's *Haunch of Venison* (Hibberd)
Mr Lawrence's *Bright Phoebus* (Mr Elwes)
Mr F Clark's *Lucy Lockitt* (Hibberd)
Mr Littler's *Firebrand* (Mr Boynton) – walkover
Mr Adkins's *Curious* (Cresswell)
Mr Lawrence's *Bright Phoebus* (Cheswass)
Mr C Fenning's *Flyaway* (Charlton)
Mr H Lewis's *Helena* (Ashmall)

1856 Mr T Stevens's *Noisette* (Yates)
Mr T Walker's *Gemma di Vergy* (Kendall)
Mr Drinkald's brother to *Grey Tommy* (Cavey)
Mr Saxon's *Ida* (Rodburn)
Mr G Drewe's *Worcester* (Wakefield)
Mr Gulliver's *Sorceress* (Bray)
Mr Dennet's *The Hartley Buck* (Fordham)
Mr Hewett's *Profile* (Rayner)
Lord Clifden's *Alembic* (A Day)
Mr T Walker's *Gemma di Vergy* (Kendall)
Mr Thelluson's *Madame Cliquot* (Cresswell)
Mr Taylor's *Fashion* (Esling)

1857 Sir J B Mills's *Flying Englishman* (Bray)
Mr T Walker's *Yaller Girl* (French)
Lord Howth's *Hobgoblin* (Snowden)
Mr J Merry's filly by *Chanticleer* out of *Baroness* (Faulkner)
Mr J Merry's *Lord of Lorn* (Aldcroft)
Mr Barber's *Jack Sheppard* (Dales)
Mr Mellish's *Rotterdam* (Custance)
Lord Clifden's *Chanoinesse* (Bray)
Mr J Merry's *Cock of the North* (Aldcroft)
Mr Greville's *Grand Duchess* (Plumb)
Mr Mellish's *Yesa* (Custance)
Mr T Walker's *Theodora* (Aldcroft)

1858 Lord Coventry's *My Niece* (Bray)
Mr Gulliver's *Verona* (Roberts)
Lord Ailesbury's *Compromise* (Pritchard)
Mr T Stevens's *Ardour* (Wells)
Lord Ailesbury's *Rosina* (Bottom)
Mr J Evans's *Clara Webster* (A Edwards)
Mr S Williams's *Knight of Kars* (Fordham)
Mr S Day's *Lady-well* (Crook)
Lord Coventry's *My Niece* (Bray)
Mr Copperthwaite's *Lady Kingston* (French)
Lord Ailesbury's *Tragedy* (Grimshaw)
Mr W Day's gelding by *Tadmor* out of *Matilda* (J Adams)

1859 Mr J Day's *Chere Amie* (Bray)
Mr Shelley's *Lifeboat* (L Snowdon)
Mr J Day's *Chere Amie* (Bray)
Mr J Day's *Brenhilda* (Bray)
Mr S Jacobs's *Eltham Beauty* (Edwards)
Captain Bayly's *Miss Eleanor* (Edwards)
Mr Capel's *Baven* (L Snowdon)
Mr Stevens's *Cynthia* (Grimshaw)
Mr La Mert's *Zitella* (Clement)
Mr Sadler's *Whimsical* (Sadler)
Sir J Hawley's *Madame Eglantine* (Wells)

Mr S Williams's *Hop Merchant* (Fordham)
Mr Saxon's colt by *Newcourt* out of *Treacherous* (Grimshaw)
Mr Angell's *Smut* (Bottom)

1860 Mr Jones's *Sunbury* (Midgley)
Sir E Hutchinson's *Sweetbread* (Entwisle)
Mr Cartwright's *Fairweather* (Charlton)
Lord Ailesbury's *Plumper* (Edwards)
Mr Morris's *Balham* (Grimshaw)
Mr H Coverdale's *Griffin* (Harrison)
Mr S Jacobs's *Amsterdam* (Aldcroft)
Capt Christie's *Spicebox* (Fordham)
Mr Nixon's *Watersprite* (Perry)
Mr J Clarke's *Sherborne* (Drewe)
Mr Lawrence's *Brine* (Grimshaw)
Mr H Castle's *Vouralak* (Edwards)
Sir C Rushout's *Conqueror* (Payne)
Mr Payne's *Tartlet* (Parsons)

1861 Mr Mellish's *Gaylad* (H Grimshaw)
Mr Merry's *The Knave* (Custance)
Mr Saxon's *Bally-Edmond* (Midgley)
Mr E Brayley's *Sycophant* (J Daley)
Mr Parry's *Memo* (J Snowden)
Mr York's *The Principal* (Whiteley)
Mr R Ten Broeck's *Santa Claus* (H Grimshaw)
Mr J Nightingale's *Esther* (H Grimshaw)
Mr Gulliver's *Tiara* (Cresswell)
Mr Jervis's *Don John* (Parsons)
Lord St Vincent's *Draghound* (Midgley)
Lord Stamford's *King of Hearts* (A French)
Capt Delme's *Bubbles* (Dowling)
Mr Astley's *Atherstone* (W Bottom)

1862 Mr Merry's filly by *Wild Dayrell* out of *Phemy* (J Grimshaw)
Mr Brayley's *Jack-in-the-Box* (S Adams)
Mr Merry's *Costa* (H Covey)
Mr Saxon's *Countess* (J Grimshaw)
Mr Greville's *Camperdown* (J Grimshaw)
Capt Grey's colt by *Fallow Buck* out of *Peace* (Dowling)
Mr John Whittaker's *King of Utopia* (Bullock)
Mr Fleming's *Lady Derby* (Daley)
Mr David's *Dominie Sampson* (Reeves)
Capt Cooper's *Soapstone* (F Adams)
Mr T Hughes's *Juliet* (D Hughes)
Mr WS Cartwright's *Ripon* (H Grimshaw)
Mr Fleming's *Lady Derby* (J Daley)
Mr T Stevens's *Violet* (Grimshaw)
Mr T Hughes's *Ironsides* (T Hughes)

1863 Mr Brayley's *Golden Dust* (Cannon)
Mr Merry's *Crisis* (H Covey)
Mr Reeves's *Topsy* (T Finch)
Mr Whittaker's *Change* (J Grimshaw)
Mr Merry's sister to *Melsonby* (H Covey)
Mr Trimmer's *Verbena* (J Grimshaw)
Mr S Thellusson's *Kingswood* (Mordan)
Mr W Hart's *Dawdle* (E Taylor)
Mr W Pearce's *Nerus* (H Grimshaw)
Lord Bateman's *Danaus* (J Grimshaw)
Mr Low's *Gibraltar* (Custance)
Mr T Hughes's *Good-for-Nothing* (F French)
Mr Reeve's *Topsy* (J Grimshaw)
Mr E Crawshaye's *Eastminster* (G Pulham)
Mr Wadlow's *Tarrangona* (G Fordham)

1864 Mr Woodson's *Deerfoot* (J Clay)
Mr R Ten Broeck's *Idler* (Fordham)
Mr Beadman's *Lord of the Manor* (Fordham)
Mr W H Mundy's *Fanny* (Fordham)
Mr Crook's *Loafer* (Fordham)

Mr S Thelluson's *Bally Edmond* (Fordham)
Capt King's *Belle of Kars* (Loates)
Mr Brayley's *Pelios* (Cannon)
Mr Payne's *Tomfoolery* (J Grimshaw)
Mr Golby's *Under the Cloud* (H Clark)
Mr G Fenwick's *Batsman* (E Forster)
Capt Cooper's *Czarina* (F Grimshaw)
Marquis of Hastings's *Lady Egidia* (Fordham)
Lord Westmoreland's *Practitioner* (Loates)
Lord Westmoreland's *Voluptas* (Fordham)
Mr Payne's *Rest* (H Grimshaw)
Mr Notley's *Clementi* (S Adams)
Prince Soltikoff's *Nebuchadnezzar* (J Grimshaw)

1865 Mr Merry's *Crisis* (Fordham)
Mr G Angell's *Lady Valentine* (Perry)
Mr Pardoe's *Qui Vive* (Custance)
Mr Ambery's *Nemo* (J Grimshaw)
Mr Godding's *Vicksburg* (Perry)
Mr E Brayley's *Pearl Diver* (Cannon)
Mr Handley's *Retrousse* (J Grimshaw)
Mr Nightingall's *Discretion* (Storey)
Mr J H C Wyndham's *The Mason* (Adams)
Mr Smith's *Hornblower* (Goater)
Mr Pardoe's *Qui Vive* (Heartfield)
Mr Hughes's *Virtuous* (Herbert)
Mr R Ten Broeck's *Reinfrid* (Barlow)
Mr T V Morgan's *The Plover* (Covey)

1866 Mr Pryor's *Troublesome* (Loates)
Mr Heathcote's *Skirmish* – walkover
Mr Brayley's *Heliotrope* (Murray)
Mrs W S Cartwright's colt by *Musjid* out of *Miss Aldcroft* (Custance)
Mr C Blanton's *A D Wagner* (Fordham)
Mr R Ten Broeck's *Usher* (Fordham)
Mr Beadman's *Aggravator* (Murray)
Mr York's *Birkdale* (H Covey)

Mr Cliff's *Alice Lee* (Fordham)
Mr R Ten Broeck's *Claymore* (Murray)
Capt Christie's *Salliet* (J Grimshaw)
Mr A C Douglas's *Miss Frances* (G Fordham)
Mr A Taylor's *Captain Kidd* (Challenor)

1867 Mr Land's *Rob Roy* (Butler)
Mr Chaplin's *Volunteer* (Custance)
Mr Payne's *Bradamante* (H Covey)
Mr R Herbert's *Balsamo* (T French)
Mr Padwick's *The Don* (Cannon)
Mr J Stephenson's *Zisca* (Heartfield)
Sir F Johnstone's *Monitor* (Maidment)
Mr Hobson's *Bandmaster*
Mr E Rickard's *Rally* (Peppler)
Mr Beadman's *Orion* (Clement)
Sir F Johnstone's *Monitor* (Maidment)
Mr T Cliff's filly by *Voltigeur* out of *Moresca* (Kenyon)
Mr Lowe's *Amour Propre* (Peppler)
Capt Christie's *Rob Roy* (Butler)
Mr Brewer's *Deceiver* (H Clarke)

1868 Mr Saxon's *Diadem* (Clement)
Mr Payne's *Victress* (Maidment)
Mr Drewitt's *Lictor* (Fordham)
Mr Padwick's *Matilda* (Fordham)
Mr Payne's *Red Ribbon* (Wilson)
Mr Naylor's *Lady Highthorn* (Kenyon)
Mr D Lawrence's *Dalwhinnie* (Kenyon)
Mr Mackenzie's *Sycee* (Cameron)
Mr T Hughes's *Paris* (Cannon)
Prince Soltykoff's *Badsworth* (J Mann)
Colonel Martin's *Fal-lal* (Kenyon)
Mr T Hughes's *Seringapatam* (Mordan)
Mr T V Morgan's *Venetia* (Butler)
Mr Edwards's *Breach of Promise* (J Edwards)

1869 Mr C Jarvis's *Little Coates* (G Jarvis)
Mr T Cliff's *Master Willie* (Kenyon)
Mr Mumford's *Lady Clinton* (Fordham)
Mr Heene's *Hawthornden* (J Adams)
Mr Merry's *Miss Hayes* (Butters)
Mr J Nightingall's *Agate* (Wyatt)
Mr J Ambrose's *Contempt* (Killick)
Lord Rendlesham's *La Rose* (Jewitt)
Mr J Lowe's *Transgressor* (J Clark)
Mr Payne's *Marshal Ney* (Mordan)
Mr R Porter's *Thunderclap* (Rowell)
Mr G Jones's *Cestus* (Fordham)
Mr Saxon's *April Morn* (Barnard)
Mr Heene's *Acorn* (Sopp)

1870 Mr Adam's *Appeal* (Newhouse)
Mr Moreton's *Vagabond* (J Adams)
Mr C Wodehouse's *Juliet* (Jewitt)
Mr G Clements's *Pretty Bird* (Lynham)
Mr W Graham's *Lizzie Cowl* (Fordham)
Mr T Hughes's *Seringpatam* (Hibberd)
Mr Graham's *Huntsman* (D Page)
Mr Graham's *Lizzie Cowl* (Fordham)
Mr T Stevens's *Lady Lavender* (Skelton)
Mr Payne's *Jester* (Chaloner)
Mr Graham's *Leazes* (Vinell)
Mr C Knight's *Panada* (Webb)

1871 Mr Merry's *Gong* (Newhouse)
Mr J Crick's *Outpost* (H Covey)
Mr W G Jarvis's *Tails* (Jeffrey)
Lord Anglesey's *Calypso* (T Cannon)
Mr Trimmer's *Moss Rose* (Killick)
Lord Anglesey's *Lampeto* (T Cannon)
Mr Dennett's *South Hatch* (R I'Anson)
Mr Payne's *Annie Wood* (Lowe)
Mr Hunt's *Duplicity* (Killick)

Mr Speedy's *Pretty Crater* (G Jarvis)
Mr J Crick's *Outpost* (H Covey)
Mr E Edwyn's *Trident* (Macksey)
Mr W Burton's *Miss Middleton* (W Bambridge)

1872 Mr Crick's *Outpost* (Hibberd)
Mr Russell's *Pelerin* (Archer)
Mr J Thomas's *Amy Roselle* (Macksey)
Lord Aylesford's *Aeropolis* (T Cannon)
Mr M'Queen's *Lady Lyon* (Mordan)
Mr G Crooks's *May Bloom* (Crowther)
Lord Howth's *Glenaveena* (T Cannon)
Mr A Poole's *Clifton* (Mr A Yates)
Lord Anglesey's *Acropolis* (T Cannon)
Mr S Jacob's *Anathema* (Barton)
Mr WG Jarvis's *Blackstone* (Jarvis)
Mr J Prince's *Marshal Prim* (Newhouse)
Mr B Water's *St George* (Huxtable)
Mr T Oliver's *Fanfaron* (Archer)
Mr T Cannon's *Rosalind* (T Cannon)

1873 Mr Newman's *Cranbourne* (T Cannon)
Mr Hureton's *Bedgown* (Constable)
Mr Ellam's *Lady Warren* (Constable)
Captain G Stirling's *Lowlander* (Mordan)
Mr Lee's *Souvenir* (Mordan)
Mr W Green's *Scottische* (J Jarvis)
Mr Schwinge's *Gnossia Corona*
Mr Lane's *Maud* (Archer)
Mr T Stevens's *Faerie* (Custance)
Mr Taylor's *Decoration* (Archer)
Mr Ellam's *Lady Warren* (Constable)
Mr JR Rone's *Oceania* (Hamshaw)
Mr Jas Dover's *Early Morn* (Archer)
Mr Schwinge's *Gnossia Corona* (Wyatt)
Mr Stevens's *Abingdon* (Hamshaw)
Mr N Green's *Schottische* (Mr Halford)

Mr I Woolcott's *Industrious* (Wyatt)
Mr T Cannon's *Pharaide* (H Day)
Mr Halford's *Santanella* (W Daniels)
Mr A Yates's *May Bush* (A Yates)
Mr R J Woodman's *Malcolm* (H Day)
Mr R Musk's *Patrician* (A May)
Mr H Ellison's *Weathercock* (H Ellison)
Mr W Burton's *Revolver* (G Mann)
Mr C S Halford's *Santanella* (W Daniels)
Mr Salt's *Worthy* (Mr Hobson)

1874 Mr Spencer's *Ashfield* (Goater)
Mr Sanders's *Hoodwink* (Morbey)
Mr J Dover's *Mary White* (Crickmere)
Mr Raymond's *Vril* (Newhouse)
Mr J Woodman's *Letty Hyde* (Giles)
Mr W K Walker's *Industrious* (Fox)
Mr W F Watson's *Valerie* (G Lowe)
Mr Morewood's *Middle Temple* (Mordan)
Mr Craufurd's *Cocotte* (W Clay)
Mr J Dover's *Early Morn* (Archer)
Mr J Dover's *Mary White* (Crickmere)
Mr J Percival's *Rattle* (Whiteley)
Mr J Cheese's *Oceania* (Archer)
Mr Raimond's *Miss Orton* (Newhouse)
Mr Hunt's *Bras de Fer* (Aldridge)
Mr F Lynham's *Juvenis* (F Lynham)
Mr E Bainbridge's *Victorious* (J Clark)
Mr J Grove's *Simplon* (Barry)
Mr Dodson's *Sir Lionel* (F Lynham)
Captain W Otway's *Tramp* (Mr Williams)
Mr Hunt's *Bras de Fer* (Aldridge)
Mr Coode's *Chancellor* (Baverstock)
Mr E W Dunn's *Stanton* (R I'Anson)
Mr T Stevens's *Mardi Gras* (Davis)
Mr T Stevens's *Flash* (E Martin)
Mr W K Walker's *Minnie Warren* (W Daniels)

Appendix C: Calcot, Whiteknights and Whitley winners

1857 Mr Wyndham's *Moetis* (Bryer)
Mr H Chinnock's *West End* (Mr Gilbert)
Mr John's *The Minor* (Stevens)
Mr W Palmer's *Fanny* (West)

1859 Mr J L Manby's *Kibworth Lass* (Enoch)
Mr B Land jnr's *Sportsman* (Owner)
Mr J L Manby's *Alfred the Great* (G Stevens)
Mr W A Wheatley's *Creeping Jane* (Best)
Mr Farmer's *Mr Somerville* (G Stevens)
Mr C Holman's *Tamworth* (Holman jnr)
Mr B Land jnr's *Sportsman* (Owner)
Mr John's *The Minor* (G Stevens)

1860 Mr Catton's *Brunette* (Kendall)
Mr Willoughby's *Profile* (English)
Mr J L Manby's *Kibworth Lass* (Enoch)
Mr Tompkins's *Jessie* (Nightingall)
Mr Peck's *Tumbler* (Nightingall)
Mr Harrison's *Omar Pasha* (G Stevens)
Mr A Howes's *Litigation* (J Land)
Mr Catton's *Brunette* (Kendall)

1861 Mr Land's Oliver *Twist* (J Land)
Capt Echalaz's *Slasher* (Mr Barry)
Mr B Land's *Red Rover* (J Land)
Mr J Manby's *Kibworth Lass* (Enoch)
Capt Williams's *Boughton* (Owner)
Mr B Land's *Red Rover* (J Land)
Mr A Howe's *Litigation* (J Land)

1862 Mr W Holman's *Sunbeam* (G Holman) – walkover
Mr B Land jnr's *Savernake* (B Land jnr)
Mr A Yates's *Playman* (Nightingall)
Mr T Duffield's *Bounce* (Owner)

Mr A Yates's *Playman* (Nightingall)
Mr Land's *Ascot* (Mr Martin)
Mr E Hayward's *The Flat* (Mr Pullen)
Mr Nightingall's *Catherine* (Nightingall)

1866 Mr P Herbert's *Whitehall* (A Sadler)
Mr Barter's *Serious Case* (Mumford)
Mr Carew's *Redwing* (Barry)
Mr Thomas's *Brunette* (Grant)
Mr F G Hobson's *Truimpher* (Owner)
Mr Oldreeve's *Lot 84* (B Land)
Mr T Hidson's *Meanwood* (J Page)
Mr Ellison's *Arlescott* (Rickaby)
Mr Barton's *Elise* (A Sadler)

1868 Mr A Yates's *Balloon* (half-bred) (Mr F G Hobson)
Mr Jarvis's *Alice Mary* (Filkins)
Mrs Percival's *Love-in-a-Mist* (Coslett)
Sir W Call's *Lawrence* (half-bred) (G Searle)
Mr Hoade's *Warwick Lass* (J Hoad)
Mr H Ellison's *The Guide* (J Rickaby)

1872 Mr H Ellison's *Rattlesnake* (Owner)
Mr A Yates's *Crawler* (Owner)
Mr J Bench's *Miss Brunel* (Potter)
Mr J Norris's *Lightning* (T Barton)
Mr Harborough's *Rho* (W Reeves)
Mr J Woodward's *Black Swan* (Potter)
Mr H Ellison's *Bob* (Crouch)
Mr T Yates's *Lawrence* (Mr A Yates)
Mr Davenport's *Barney* (Stripp) – walkover
Mr Perry's *King of the Roses* (Mr Bambridge)
Mr Henwood's *Honfleur* (Silk) – walkover
Mr R Todd's *Vivandiere* (Mr Goodwin)
Baron Finot's *Cinna* (Mr Yates)
Mr A Yates's *Crawler* (Owner)
Mr Warne's horse by *Prime Minister* (W Jarvis) – walkover

Mr W H Johnstone's *Chance* (Owner)
Mr W H Johnstone's *Chance* (Owner)
Mr J Stratton's *St Kilda* (Sutton)
Baron Finot's *Martin* (Mr A Yates)
Mr Wheatley's *Miss Raggy* (Mr FR Godwin)
Mr J Nightingall's *Dora* (R I'Anson)
Mr Rickard's *Trifle* (Wheeler)
Mr W H Johnstone's *Chance* (Owner)

1873 Mr A Yates's *Mustapha* (Owner)
Mr Doncaster's *Scrub* (Mr J Goodwin)
Mr J Percival's *Owen Swift* (Whiteley)
Mr W G Jarvis's *Guide* (Gregory)
Mr A Yates's *Crawler* (Owner)
Mr James Nightingall's *St Valentine* (Wyatt)
Mr H Ellison's *Optima* (Owner)
Mr H Ellison's *Rattlesnake* (R I'Anson)
Mr Mumford's *Little Doctor* (Owner)
Mr A Yates's *Ashmour* (Owner)

1874 Mr R Allday's *Wasp* (Gillett)
Capt Oliphant's *John O'Groat* (W Reeves)
Mr A Poole's *Judge* (W Bambridge)
Mr H Ellison's *Sultana* (Bagley)
Mr H Ellison's *Huntsman* (Bagley)
Mr H J Simonds's *Bismarck* (Capt Clifton)
Mr J Allen's *Saracen* (Carroll)
Mr G Bracher's *Victorire* (Mr Barnes)
Maj Wortham's *Gay Lad* (Mr Crawshaw)
Mr F J Main's *Roue* (J North)
Mr Hureton's *Partridge* (R I'Anson)

1875 Mr Jno Bambrudge's *The Maze* (J Cassidy)
Mr A Yates's *Harvester* (Mr Barnes)
Mr Forster's *Ely Dorado* (Mr H Hobson)
Mr J Percival's *Sunny* (Gregory)
Mr E W Dunn's *Stanton* (W Daniels)
Mr W H Johnstone's *My Lady* (Owner)
Mr J Percivals's *Sparrow* (Gregory)
Mr T Drax's *David Copperfield* (Mr FG Hobson)
Mr Hargreaves's *Miss Hardcastle* (Mr Baldwin)
Mr Humphrey's *Frialty* (Gregory)
Mr Ward's *Melly* (Comber)
Mr Rawdon's *Jorrocks* (W Reeves)
Mr J Bambridge's *The Maze* (J Cassidy)
Capt Whyte's *Outpost* (Comber)

Appendix D: Maiden Erlegh winners

1886 Mr C E Pigott's *Pleasure Boat* (Owner)
Corp Ayres's *My Girl* (Owner)
Mr R T Hermon Hodge's *Convoy* (Mr Johnson)
Major Spiller's *Dressmaker* (Mr Waller)
Mr C E Pigott's *Pleasure Boat* (Owner)
Mr F E Lawrence's *Honeycomb* (Owner)

1887 Mr C E Pigott's *Playlight* (late *My Girl*) (Owner)
Mr G Ireland jnr's *Hogarth* (T Skelton)
Mr Tyrone's *Riven Oak* (A Hall)
Mr J Hargreaves Jnr's *Surprise* (Owner)
Mr C E Pigott's *Playlight* (Owner)
Mr G Ayres's *Gambler* (Owner)

1888 Mr G Ayres's *Farmer Jack* (Owner)
Mr F Headington's *Billy Pepper* (Mr W Pullen)
Mr W A Bristow's *Fresh Start* (Mr Bewicke)
Mr G Ayres's *Kit* (Capt E R Owen)
Mr E Benson's *Kilworth* (Capt E R Owen)
Mr E A Coldicutt's *His Lordship* (Mr A Wheatley)

1889 Mr G Ayres's *Kit* (Owner)
Mr J A Bristow's *Fresh Start* (Mr Saunders)
Mr D Thirwell's *Wingstock* (Halsey)
Mr A Wheatley's *Silver Star* (Capt E R Owen)
Mr Ashday's *Cabin Boy* (Capt E R Owen)
Mr W G Flanagan's *Miss Hastings* (Mr A Wheatley)

1890 Mr J C Dormer's *B Flat* (Guy)
Mr E E Hanbury's *Climbaxe* (Mr Slade)
Mr Swan's *Southam* (Dollery)
Mr W G Flanagan's *Miss Hastings* (Mr G Ayres)
Mr Swan's *Mushroon* (Owner)
Mr T Cannon's *Poorago* (Mawson)

1891 Capt Bewick's *Plank* (Owner)
Mr W H Gard's *Nap* (Mr W Pullen)
Mr Abington's *Edio* (Capt E R Owen)
Mr R T Hermon-Hodge's *Lady Evelyn* (Capt Frith)
Mr Gunnis's *Anaconda* (Capt J D Barry)
Mr Abington's *Isleworth* (Mr W Pullen)

1892 Mr R T Hermon-Hodge's *Lady Evelyn* (Capt Frith)
Mr J C Dormer's *Ordeal* (Owner)
Mr Swan's Bay *Comus* (W Dollery)
Mr H L Powell's *Haddington* (Dollery)
Mr G A Clements's *Westcote* (A Clement)
Mr A Wheatley's *Decoy* (Mr C E Pigott)

1893 Mrs Ella Donovan's *Cushalee* (Oliver)
Lord Dangan's *Knighthood* (Owner)
Mr Swan's *Dutch Hoe* (Mr H M Ripley)
Lord Dangan's *Ninepins* (Owner)
Mr J C Dormer's *Dora* (Mr Withington) – walkover
Mr W C Keeping's *Biscuit* (Mr W Pullen)

1894 Mr W Garrard's *Bainacoil* (Owner)
Sir J Dickson-Poynder's *Brookwood* (Mr W Lindsay)
Mr W C Keeper's *Biscuit* (W Pullen)
Mr G Russell's *Daffodil* (Mr C Payne)
Sir J Dickson-Poynder's *Nellie* (Mr W Lindsay)
Miss Langworthy's *The Pawn* (Mr Ricardo)

1895 Mr Oliver Dixon's *Cushalee II* (Mr Tennant)
Mr J Adamthwaite's *Ben Night* (Mr J T Brain)
Mr W C Keeping's *Anchor* (Matthews)
Mr W C Clack's *Skelton* (Mr C Clack)
Mr W C Keeping's *Greenhill* (Matthews)
Mr W C Keeping's *Biscuit* (Capt Beevor)

1896 Mr Oliver Dixon's *Cushalee Machree* (Mr Gundry)
Mr E H Polehampton's *Sting* (P Sherlock)
Mr R Gore's *Elinor* (Collard)
Mr G C Scruby's *Ringabella* (Mr G Bellilue)
Mr H C Simonds's *The Orphan* (T Holland)
Mr G C Scruby's *Rockfield* (J Jones)

1897 Mr Jno Hewett's *Tim Bobbin* (Mr D Lewis)
Mr E O Bleakley's *I.O.U.* (T Fitton) – walkover
Mr F Swan's *Miss Horner* (E Acres)
Mr R Gore's *Inigo* (W Clement)
Mr H Sidney's *Gangbridge* (Owner)
Mr H G Lukie's *Loddon* (Ebenezer Hunt)

1898 Mr G C Roller's *Marvellous* (Owner)
Mr E H Polehampton's *Sting* (P Sherlock)
Major Hughes Onslow's *Melton Constable* (Owner)
Mr F Price Brown's *Spitfire* (Faulkner)
Miss Skinner's *Dolly May* (E Acres)
Mr W H Lambton's *Romanoff* (Owner)

1899 Mr H Caversham Simonds's *Fortune* (Mr C Garrard)
Mr E H Polehampton's *Sting* (P Sherlock) – walkover
Mr H E Elwes's *Corabie* (Owner)
Mr A Wheatley's *Honey Bee* (Mr French Davis)
Mr T Leader's *Dorado* (T Leader jnr)
Mr J Summers's Britain's *Glory* (W Raymond)

1900 Mr Garrett Moore's *Herne* (Mr F Hartigan)
Mr Chilcott's *Gribon* (Dollery)
Mr H Caversham Simonds's *Horoscope* (Clack)
Mr R C Dawson's *Zelie* (O'Brien)
Mr W Harris's *Corner* (W Nye)
Capt A Hill's *Sweet Viola* (W Nye)
Mt T Leader's *Artiste* (T Leader jnr)

1901 Major J D Edwards's *Edwardine* (Mason)
Mr F L Wilson's *Livorno* (R Gordon)
Mr B D McCulloch's *Monotype* (Dollery)
Mr S B Joel's *Uncle Jack* (Mr Hartigan)
Mr W Harris's *Germanicus* (W Nye)
Mr H J Hall's *Killeenleigh* (O'Brien)
Mr H Barnato's *Prosset* (Mr Hartigan)
Mr H B Blagrave's *Belle Magnifique* (Matthews)
Mr R C Dawson's *Mill Girl* (O'Brien)
Mr W Sibary's *Trustee* (Dollery)
Mr Pape's *Mack Briggs* (G Armstrong)
Mr J Craig's *Scoundrel* (E Matthews)
Mr A Gordon's *Red Friar II* (Owner)
Mr P Gourflay's *Issa* (J Stainton)
Mr W Lotinga's *Marriage Lines* (A Birch)
Mr J E Barnett's *Sanctissima II* (F Mason)
Mr Part's *Squint II* (Mr A Hastings)
Mr S B Joel's *Sly Fox* (Mr A Hastings)
Mr S B Joel's *Mintstalk* (Mr F Hartigan)
Mr E C Lovegrove's *Revera* (W Hopkins)
Mr C H Styles's *Golden Sally* (H Adams) – walkover
Mr C Habin's *Bowsprit* (Owner)

1902 Mr S B Joel's *Gorgonzola* (Gowland)
M N Burton's *Marcha Real* (A Nightingall)
Mr T Sutcliffe's *Gaylord* (Gowland)
Mr Rhodes's *Mereclough* (T Fitton)
Mr H Barnato's *Prosset* (Gowland)
Mr H Turner's *Irish Linen* (G F Wilson)
Mr O E Part's *Titus II* (Mr Hastings)
Mr J Ivall's *Bell Magnifique* (J Stainton)
Mr W McAuliffe's *Coolock* (H Buxton)
Mr R D Hill's *Morglette* (Piggott)
Mr O Dixon's *Tatcho* (Mr Rogers)
Mr George Parker's *Mercury II* (A Parker)
Mr G Gully's *Sal Volatile* (Mr G C Nugent)
Mr B Parker's *Tyninghame* (F Barratt)

Major Caversham Simonds's *Gentle Hilda* (Mr J T Rogers)
Mr C E Mason's *Darner* (J O'Brien)
Mr R Gore's *Red Friar II* (F Mason)
Mr H Bonas's *Owenmore* (F Mason)
Mr W Shaw's *Miss Royston* (A Newey)
Mr F R Hunt's *Billy George* (E Matthews)
Mr E P Ryan's *Runaway Girl* (E Sullivan)
Mr C D Barrow's *Gillie II* (Mr GC Nugent)
Mr H T Mills's *Bella Angela* (Owner)

1903 Mr L W Winans's *Ragamuffin* (J Barrett)
Mr Deer's *Sir Francis Drake* (Owner)
Mr J H Locke's *Mahratta* (W Dollery)
Mr T E Hunt's *Rosy Glen* (J Hunt)
Mr W Bird's *Blagueur* (E Southwood)
Sir J Blundell Maple's *Grandchild* (C Horan)
Mr A Hastings's *Titus II* (Owner)
Mr G M Stevens's *Cookham* (Donnelly)
Mr F W Polehampton's *Saleratus* (F Freemantle)
Mr J C H Lucy's *Roman Bath* (Mr Deer)
Mr A D H Law's *Little Brown Mouse* (Mr A Hastings)
Mr S B Joel's *Marcha Real* – walkover
Mr R Lake's *South America* (H Garratt)
Mr T Southall's *Cherokee* (Newey)
Mr S B Joel's *Mintstalk* (Mason)
Mr F R Fry's *Hampton Court* (T Dunn)
Mr T Southall's *Lyndon Green* (Newey)
Mr W Bird's *Blagueur* (Mr Nugent)
Mr W B Partridge's *Spread Eagle* (D Morgan)
Mr W R Clarke's *Bella Angela* (H Woodland)
Mr J Bancroft's *Favonius* (T Fitton)
Mr Lort Phillip's *Friary* (Mason)
Mr J Bristowe's *Campanone* (A Nightingall)
Mr H G Johnson's *Kladderadatch* (T Fitton)

1904 Mr S B Joel's *Uncle Jack* (F Hartigan)
Mr H Bonas's *Copt Heath* (F Freemantle)
Mr L F Craven's *Vibrant* (R Woodland)
Mr R Gore's *Lady Belge* (Mason)
Mr J E Stevens's *Uphantes* (Owner)
Mr F M Freake's *Lavender Kid* (Magee)
Capt R H Collis's *Carnroe* (Owner)
Mr W Pullen's *Lady Malta* (Mr Billycald)
Mr J C Sullivan's *Atrocious* (F Mason)
Mr A Gordon's *Do Not Forget* (Owner)
Mr W F Stratton's *Portside* (Owner)
Mr P Whittaker's *Brian Boru* (Owner)
Capt D M Miller's *Ballin O'Monk* (Mr A Gordon)
Col T Brinckman's *Venom* (Acres)
Mr W R Pickett's *Garter Knight* (M E Hampton)
Gen Sir Bruce Hamilton's *Olive* (Capt Rasbotham)
Mr S B Joel's *Mintstalk* (Mason)
Mr H Lindemere's *Craig Dhu* (Owner)
Mr P Whitaker's *The Lawyer III* (Owner)
Mr S B Joel's *His Lordship* (F Hartigan)
Mr C Wood's *Matchboard* (Mr Barthropp)
Mr C D Barrow's *Gillie II* (Wilkins)
Mr T W Pratt's *Sea Gal* (A Magee)
Mr C H Style's *Monster* (F Reed)
Lord Montgomerie's *Ellaline II* (R Gordon)
Mr T J Longworth's *Chilumchee* (Savage)
Mr A Wilson's *Monster* (T Dunn)
Mr F C Burroughs's *Sudden Rise* (A Pratt)
Mr F Prichard's *Grandchild* (F Lyall)
Mr J T Raisin's *Susanna* (F Mason)
Mr W P Allen's *I Know* (Magee)

1905 Mr G H Freeman's *Norham* (Hammond)
Mr H Bonas's *Buck Up* (Clancy)
Mr R Courage's *World's Desire* (T Dunn)
Mr C Wilkinson's *Young Neville* (G Goswell)
Mr H Lines's *Bird of Treasure* (W C Tabor)
Mr G Parker's *Furzey Common* (Parker)
Mr T Clyde's *Colnard* (O'Brien)
Mr Bonas's *Catherine Green* (Freemantle)
Mr R W Clarke's *Intaglio* (Mr H Fitt)
Mr H M Dyas's *Wych Elm* (E Ward)
General Hamilton's *Olive* (Mr W Bulteel)
Mr F U Webb's *Celebration* (R Gordon)
Mr J P Arkwright's *Cortina* (D Faulkner)
Mr R Gore's *Hi Hi* (Clancy)
Mr T Sherwood's *Call Duck* (L Sherwood)
Mr T Lumley-Smith's *Alert II*I (Owner)
Mr C Douglas-Pennant's *Amabit* (C Horne)
Mr John Widger's *Royal Bow* (Mr H Rich)
Mr George Parker's *Little Tom* (Parker)
Mr J North's *Wild Gander* (Fitton)
Mr Delegarde's *Richmond Boy* (A Cole)
Mr J F Hallick's *Addlestone* (E Matthews)
Maj P G Reynold's *Quiff* (O'Brien)
Mr J F Hallick's *Lord Cork* (E Matthews)

1906 Mr H M Hartigan's *Severna* (F Morgan)
Maj F C Stratton's *Storm King* (Capt Rasbotham)
Mr H M Hartigan's *Irish Angel* (F Morgan)
Mr John Coleman's *Morocco Bound* (W Palmer)
Mr H M Hartigan's *Cissy's Revel* (Mr W Bulteel)
Mr D R Aikman's *New Norfolk* (Mr W Bulteel)
Mr C Bewicke's *Triplands* (Whiley)
Mr John Colman's *Morocco Bound* (Palmer)
Mr D Wells's *Arcadic* (J Conway)
Mr R C de Crespigny's *Wedding Tour* (Rollison)
Mr A Poole's *Bob Sawyer* (Mr Poole)
Mr C N Manning's *Sonning* (Rollison)

Bibliography

Bayles, F. H. *The Race Courses Atlas of Great Britain & Ireland.* London: Henry Faux, 1903

Boyd, David *The Running Horses: a brief history of racing in Berkshire from 1740.* Berkshire County Libraries, 1978

Earley Local History Group *Earley Days: an illustrated account of our community's development.* Reading: ELHG, 2000

Graham, Clive & Curling, Bill *The Grand National: an illustrated history of the greatest steeplechase in the world.* London: Barrie and Jenkins, 1972

Joel, Stanhope *Ace of Diamonds: The story of Solomon Barnato Joel as told to Lloyd Mayer.* London: Frederick Muller, 1958

Magee, Sean *Ascot: the history.* London: Methuen, 2002

Mitford, Mary Russell *Belford Regis; or, Sketches of a country town.* London: T. Werner Laurie, 1942

Mortimer, Roger, Onslow, Richard & Willett, Peter *Biographical Encyclopaedia of British Flat Racing.* London: Macdonald and Jane's, 1978

Pitt, Chris *A Long Time Gone.* Rev. ed. Halifax: Portway, 2006

Passages from the diaries of Mrs. Philip Lybbe Powys of Hardwick House, Oxon: A.D. 1756–1808. Edited by Emily J. Climenson. London: Longmans, Green, and Co., 1899

Seth-Smith, Michael et al *The History of Steeplechasing.* London: M. Joseph, 1969

Stokes, Penelope *Free Rein: Racing in Berkshire and beyond 1700–1905* Newbury: P. Stokes, 2005

Tanner, Michael & Cranham, Gerry *The Guinness Book of Great Jockeys of the Flat: a celebration of two centuries of jockeyship.* Enfield, Guinness, 1992

Wright, Howard *Encyclopedia of Flat Racing.* 2nd ed. London: Robert Hale, 1986

Berkshire Chronicle

Reading Observer

Reading Mercury

Bell's Sporting Life

Racing Illustrated

Racing Calendar